# Essentials for New Principals

# Essentials for New Principals

## Seven Steps to Becoming Successful—Key Expectations and Skills

Richard D. Sorenson

ROWMAN & LITTLEFIELD
Lanham • Boulder • New York • London

Published by Rowman & Littlefield
An imprint of The Rowman & Littlefield Publishing Group, Inc.
4501 Forbes Boulevard, Suite 200, Lanham, Maryland 20706
www.rowman.com

86-90 Paul Street, London EC2A 4NE, United Kingdom

Copyright © 2023 by Richard D. Sorenson

*All rights reserved.* No part of this book may be reproduced in any form or by any electronic or mechanical means, including information storage and retrieval systems, without written permission from the publisher, except by a reviewer who may quote passages in a review.

British Library Cataloguing in Publication Information available

**Library of Congress Cataloging-in-Publication Data**

Names: Sorenson, Richard D., author.
Title: Essentials for new principals : seven steps to becoming successful, key expectations and skills / Richard D. Sorenson.
Description: Lanham : Rowman & Littlefield, 2023. | Includes bibliographical references and index. | Summary: "Essentials for New Principals: Seven Steps to Becoming Successful - Key Expectations and Skills is written for new and aspiring principals who desire to gain specialized skills, knowledge, and expertise associated with the incorporation of seven essential steps all related to the advancement of key expectations and critical skills by means of academically-sound and research-based leadership processes thus, ensuring leadership success"—Provided by publisher.
Identifiers: LCCN 2023022006 (print) | LCCN 2023022007 (ebook) | ISBN 9781475871890 (cloth) | ISBN 9781475871906 (paperback) | ISBN 9781475871913 (epub)
Subjects: LCSH: School principals—In-service training—United States. | Educational leadership—United States. | School management and organization—United States. | Teacher-principal relationships—United States.
Classification: LCC LB1738.5 .S67 2023  (print) | LCC LB1738.5 (ebook) | DDC 371.2/012—dc23/eng/20230524
LC record available at https://lccn.loc.gov/2023022006
LC ebook record available at https://lccn.loc.gov/2023022007

*To my wife for being a remarkable and constant source of love and always been there with support, wisdom, knowledge, and expertise. Over the years, project after project, she has been my secret weapon, always believing in me and willing to assist me. She has poured hours into this book with me, discussing the pages, reading draft after draft, offering edit recommendations, and always providing sound advice and good ideas. This book is dedicated to you, Donna—you are the love of my life!*

*And to Steve,
my ninety-one-year-old valued friend!
Your good nature, great humor, and indomitable spirit
regularly enliven me, and I'll always be grateful.
You may be in your ninety-first year of life, but
you continue to remain young at heart!*

# Contents

Acknowledgments ix

Introduction xi

Chapter 1: The New Principal: The Administrative Role—Then and Now 1

Chapter 2: Step #1: Advance Critical New Principal Skills: Develop a Plan for Success 17

Chapter 3: Step #2: The Leadership Absolutes Vital to Confidently Experiencing Today's Principalship: Part 1: How to Identify, Acknowledge, and Incorporate the Seven Absolutes Essential to New Principal Success 35

Chapter 4: Step #2: The Leadership Absolutes Vital to Confidently Experiencing Today's Principalship: Part 2: Absolute #7: How to Successfully Endure, Transcend, and Survive the Seven Emergent Forces Challenging the New Principal Role 51

Chapter 5: Step #3: Learn the Ropes: New Principal Expectations, Position Responsibilities, and Skill Sets to Positively Influence New Principal Leadership 69

Chapter 6: Step #4: Acknowledge and Understand School Norms, Traditions, and Customs: What New Principals Must Know to Survive 83

Chapter 7: Step #5: Recognize and Value Essential Characteristics of the Learning Community: Factors New Principals Must Know and Understand 101

Chapter 8: Step #6: Appreciate and Incorporate Policies, Regulations, and Procedures: New Principal Legal Responsibilities     117

Chapter 9: Step #7: Enhance Personal Attributes Critical to a New Principal's Success: The Leadership Protocol     129

References     137

Index     145

About the Author     153

# Acknowledgments

Always, a debt of gratitude and appreciation is extended to Tom Koerner, former vice president/senior editor, education division, of The Rowman & Littlefield Publishing Group, Inc. I am most appreciative to Tom for the writing opportunities. Also, a shout-out to Carlie Wall, managing editor, and Jasmine Holman, assistant acquisitions editor, for their behind-the-scenes prepublication work conducted on my behalf. My thanks and gratitude to all three!

### FRONT COVER DESIGN

Like a majestic tree, the new principal, step-
by-step, must put down deep roots
and grow strong to withstand those ever-prevailing
and constantly changing conditions
that often doggedly bend yet never break a determined leader.

# Introduction

Principal "resignation" and "retirement": Those are perhaps the two most subjugating words in school systems today.
From a human resources perspective, new principals must be a professional recourse.
(Personnel director from a Southwest school district)
Far too many school principals lead professional lives of quiet desperation. When resignations or retirements occur, exasperation is confirmed.
New principals are often the most viable answer.
(Principal mentor and coach, Houston, Texas)
—The New Principal Test—
Am I doing the right thing at the right time in the right way for the right reason?
(Stephanie McConnel, *Principal Principles*, 2017)

Welcome to the book *Essentials for New Principals: Seven Steps to Becoming Successful—Key Expectations and Skills*. The term "new," utilized throughout the text in reference to principals, is incorporated to identify those principals who are actually beginning principals—those in their first year as a school leader.

The postpandemic era is in full swing. Retirements, resignations, and reassignments abound. For many professionals—principals included—working from home is not only in vogue but frequently considered an approved means of production. For others, principals included, it is and has previously been absolute drudgery.

The school principalship may not be in crisis, but it is definitely in trouble! Reasoning: Principals are exiting the profession in record numbers and thus leaving new principals in place to fill and fulfill the leadership roles. Principals, much like thousands of other professionals across the nation, are leaving their positions in the wake of what has become known as the "Great Resignation."

Consider the following: In 2022, RAND Corporation found that 40 percent of school principals are planning to leave their position. The National Association of Secondary School Principals identified reasons for the great exodus: stressful working conditions, politicization of education, staff shortages, threats to principal safety, mental health needs, and the well-being of principals (Superville, 2023).

The heightened attrition and causes for such are a real concern. Retirements are as high as 23 percent postpandemic compared to 16 percent prepandemic, with one study indicating the principal prepandemic retirement rate to be as low as 3 percent, a skeptical number. The National Council for Education Statistics found that only 10 percent of principals were retiring prepandemic (Superville, 2023). These numbers are more than concerning and begs a question: Will the trend continue?

So, why do principals no longer want the job? Good question. Many would say that facing reality is what has sparked the Great Resignation. What is an absolute: A significant percentage of the new principals who are recruited to replace retiring or resigning principals are inexperienced, unseasoned, poorly prepared, inadequately trained, and, simply but sadly put, ill equipped to assume the key administrative role.

Added to the noted complexity of quality principals exiting the profession is an ongoing shortage of qualified new principals in addition to a serious teacher shortage. All of this is further compounded by an even more serious substitute teacher scarcity. These concerns are trending, and not in a positive way. All are negatively impacting student learning and achievement and, at best, complicating new principal decision-making and problem-solving capabilities. To further compromise the current situation, university principal-preparation programs are experiencing setbacks in recruiting serious-minded, competent, and capable future administrative leaders.

What is pushing principals to leave the profession and vacate their office by either resignation or retirement? Identified are the top three reasons principals are departing the field of educational administration. Principals are (1) seeking other opportunities because of overwhelming working conditions in their current administrative job; (2) finding other positions in which they are much more enthusiastic and less stressed; and (3) seeking a position with better pay and benefits, accompanied by fewer expectations and responsibilities (Ruggirello, 2022).

One resigning principal recently shared with his university principal-preparation program professor a profoundly telling letter of resignation, which was typed out and submitted with date and signature as follows: "Dear Sirs, I QUIT! Sincerely, . . ." So, as principals resign or retire, who is left holding the bag? Answer: new principals!

Now, a more pertinent question: Why has the recruiting and retaining of new principals become such an arduous and complex dilemma? There is an answer worthy of consideration. Recruiting and retaining new principals has become a challenge for several reasons, but the most significant explanation relates to new principals who are deficient in, if not completely lacking, critical attributes, key expectations, and an essential skill set for leadership success.

Today, what is required to aid these new principals in overcoming personal and professional deficiencies is a series of crucial steps, as identified in *Essentials for New Principals: Seven Steps to Becoming Successful—Key Expectations and Skills*. Fundamental to ensuring that new principals have successful leadership experiences are seven specific steps, which are identified, clarified, exemplified, and amplified in what could certainly serve as a most informative, instructive, and compelling text.

Therefore, the text is all about (1) focusing on leadership steps related to a successful new principalship by means of key expectations and skills; (2) understanding the administrative role; (3) advancing critical leadership skills; (4) incorporating leader absolutes; (5) transcending emergent forces; (6) learning new principal expectations and responsibilities; (7) understanding school norms, traditions, and customs; (8) valuing essential characteristics or factors of a learning community; (9) appreciating and incorporating policies, regulations, and procedures; and (10) enhancing all through a leadership development protocol.

- Chapter 1, "The New Principal: The Administrative Role—Then and Now," presents an introduction to the new principalship, both yesterday and today, asking the question: Has anything changed but the date on the calendar? Four critical attributes to becoming a successful new principal are identified and examined.
- Chapter 2, "Step #1: Advance Critical New Principal Skills: Develop a Plan for Success," explores five plan-of-action considerations and examples essential to a new principal finding legitimate personal success as a school leader. Moreover, critical leader skills are identified as well as practical methods of skills acquisition. Fifteen "how-to" gain leadership skills and seven keys to personal growth and development as a new principal are detailed. Additionally, the means by which a new school leader can overcome isolation are examined.
- Chapter 3, "Step #2: The Leadership Absolutes Vital to Confidently Experiencing Today's Principalship, Part 1: How to Identify, Acknowledge, and Incorporate the Seven Absolutes Essential to New Principal Success," discloses how a new principal acknowledging and utilizing seven leadership absolutes can recognize and overcome career

obstacles. Additionally, seven significant emergent forces impacting new principal leadership and success are identified to be further examined, analyzed, and studied in chapter 4.

- Chapter 4, "Step #2: The Leadership Absolutes Vital to Confidently Experiencing Today's Principalship, Part 2: Absolute #7: How to Successfully Endure, Transcend, and Survive the Seven Emergent Forces Challenging the New Principal Role," addresses seven emerging forces impacting education today and how new principals must be prepared to endure, survive, and succeed.

  The forces are (1) Pandemic Aftereffects; (2) Teacher Shortages, Quiet Quitting, and the Great Resignation; (3) Activist Parents; (4) Incivility, the Lack of Public Decorum, and Survival Tactics; (5) Technology Redefined: The Age of Digital Leading, Teaching, and Learning—Innovative Today, Obsolete Tomorrow!; (6) Social Media Effects; and (7) Controversial Issues affecting new principal leadership.

- Chapter 5, "Step #3: Learn the Ropes: New Principal Expectations, Position Responsibilities, and Skill Sets to Positively Influence New Principal Leadership," reveals an in-depth description and examination of new principal expectations. New principal position responsibilities are identified along with distinguishable differences between expectations and responsibilities. Additionally, seven key skills to positively influence new principal leadership are reviewed, as well as what makes for an outstanding new principal.

- Chapter 6, "Step #4: Acknowledge and Understand School Norms, Traditions, and Customs: What New Principals Must Know to Survive," prompts the reader to better understand and acknowledge the meaning and purpose of school norms, traditions, and customs, with each term being defined, described, and exemplified. Specific institutionally perpetual norms, traditions, and customs are a focus of the chapter, along with new principal methods of initiating change.

  Furthermore, ten steps to creating a positive school climate and open culture are listed and how a new principal can, by means of seven tactics, survive the challenge of making changes. Finally, five new principal pitfalls that can lead to career derailment are assessed.

- Chapter 7, "Step #5: Recognize and Value Essential Characteristics of the Learning Community: Factors New Principals Must Know and Understand," promotes the roles and responsibilities of the learning community members and defines essential learning community characteristics.

  In addition, the chapter identifies four fundamental factors that impact a new principal's relationship with a learning community along with what a new principal must do and not do when attempting to develop a rapport and establish a relationship with the learning community.

Additionally, five key tenets central to a new principal establishing an effective learning community and building a positive first impression are presented. Finally, the 7 Bs to a new principal overcoming failure in order to succeed are offered.

- Chapter 8, "Step #6: Appreciate and Incorporate Policies, Regulations, and Procedures: New Principal Legal Responsibilities," examines new principal legal obligations and/or requirements from the perspective of school board policies, administrative regulations, and campus procedures. Each is defined and characterized.
- Chapter 9, "Step #7: Enhance Personal Attributes Critical to a New Principal's Success: The Leadership Protocol," investigates—by means of eight multiple-choice queries—whether a new principal is driven, diplomatic, dedicated, or a combination of two or more of the noted profile indicators.

Special features of the book include the following:

- Vignettes/scenarios within each chapter applicable to new principal leadership
- "Pause and Consider" questions
- New principal leadership protocol and self-reflective learning instrument
- Discussion questions
- Case study applications and questions at the conclusion of each chapter
- References

The book is suitable for self and group book studies, workshop presentations, education courses, and professional development sessions. The target audiences are new principals and prospective K–12 administrators, as well as graduate students enrolled in university principal-preparation programs.

*Essentials for New Principals: Seven Steps to Becoming Successful—Key Expectations and Skills* is designed to offer crucial information and decisive steps providing new principals with significant competencies, important proficiencies, and vital expectations and skills to best ensure success. As a new or prospective principal, welcome to the rich and descriptive methods instilled within these pages—all essential to leading a school. Finally, enjoy the read!

*Chapter 1*

# The New Principal

## *The Administrative Role— Then and Now*

>Patiently you mentor and lead
>ShaRing wIsdom and meeting each need
>Support aNd adviCe you willIngly supply
>Upon you the faculty and puPils Anxiously reLy.
>(Anonymous)

### THE NEW PRINCIPAL OF YESTERYEAR

Fifty-plus years ago, Stephen P. Hencley, Lloyd E. McCleary, and J. H. McGrath wrote the seminal text *The Elementary School Principalship* (1970), which brought to the forefront of school leadership literature newly refined and time-tested principal research, general theoretical perspectives and constructs, administrative management techniques, and practical methods for guiding a school. The text was a companion volume to *Secondary School Administration* (1965). The new text was intended not only to illuminate problems and practices in school administration, albeit at the elementary school level, but also to reveal future essential leadership requirements and much-needed principalship development expressly for new principals.

To read each of the noted texts today readily brings forth a critical question: Has anything changed in the field of administrative leadership other than the date on the calendar? Such a query is not only significant, but the associated answer is complicated. The three co-authors, Hencley, McCleary, and McGrath, have left a positive and lasting imprint on educational leadership. Their legacy remains, yet the inquisitive mind cannot help but return to the proposed question: Has anything really changed in the field of administrative leadership other than the date on the calendar?

First, readers must return to those two groundbreaking texts, *The Elementary School Principalship* (1970) and its precursor, *Secondary School Administration* (1965), and consider what were topics of key consideration those fifty-plus years past? Examine a list from the table of contents of the 1970 text and determine which items continue today as absolutes to new principal success. Also consider what aspects of school leadership are missing from the list yet must be absolutes today.

- Administrative functions and related leader behaviors
- Programs and personnel
- Management and operations
- The principal and the profession
- Program supervision and evaluation
- Emergent forces and extending educational opportunity

Does the list match the role and responsibility of the new principal today? The author of this text would contend that the answer is both yes and no. Yes, simply because there are definitely administrative functions, clearly delineated in school systems across the nation along with associated new principal behaviors and expectations, that are institutional norms and standard district administrative practices.

Certainly, as was the case in 1965 and 1970, new principals must understand instructional programs and how personnel are trained, through professional development, to implement curricular guides and teaching strategies, techniques, and methods. Moreover, it can be agreed that principal preparation programs, as in the past, continue to teach proper new principal management and operations techniques.

Now the "no" answer relative to the proposed question: Does the previous list match the roles and responsibilities of the new principal today? To be clear, the new principal role and associated responsibilities have appropriately moved toward one of instructional leadership and, as such, has become a widely recognized and rigorously mandated new principal expectation.

Today, as was not necessarily the case in the identified texts of yesteryear, new principals must adapt to a professional mission that places excellence in learning and achievement first and foremost. True, in comparison to decades past, new school leaders must be adept in identifying emergent forces in education that can and will impact teaching, leading, and learning.

Yet, is the extending of educational opportunity to all students any different today than was the case in the late 1960s or early 1970s? Furthermore, are the emergent forces in education currently different from those in the past? Pertinent questions, challenging answers. Certainly, both questions and answers are worthy of serious consideration if not debate. Consider the following scenario and then respond to the associated questions.

### "HAPPENSTANCE IT IS NOT!"

Pierre Boulle, superintendent of Burma School System, sat in his office and shared the following with one of his associate superintendents, Sessue Hayakawa: "During my time in education, I've been fortunate enough to witness exceptional school leaders transform the fortunes of young people who are in their care. These principals, many of whom were new to the position, worked tirelessly to bring to fruition the hopes, dreams, and aspirations of many students, no matter their background or circumstance, so each student could fulfill their potential."

Superintendent Boulle went on to say, "Happenstance it is not. I don't believe such occurs by chance, coincidence, or luck, but rather because these school leaders personally developed key skills and qualities which enabled them to enhance school climates and cultures in which all members of the learning community were able to thrive, achieve, and succeed. Think about Ann Sears, our new principal over at Phillip Toosey School. She may be recent to the position, but Ann has developed, early in her time as principal, those skills, qualities, and critical attributes essential to her becoming a successful school principal."

Sessue Hayakawa, the associate superintendent, smiled, thought about what his superintendent had communicated regarding attributes of successful new principals, and then said: "Yes, sir, you are correct. Successful new principal leadership is not a fluke." Sessue went on to share what he believed were key factors to Principal Sears's success. He noted what he had observed as elements of Ann's accomplishment as a new school principal. He also suggested that these attributes should be shared and developed with each of the district's new principals.

Superintendent Boulle then asked Sessue to elaborate. Sessue began with a list of four keys, qualities, or attributes essential to becoming a successful new principal. Examine the list below and then respond to the Pause and Consider questions that follow.

\_\_\_\_ Learn the role expectations and accept position responsibilities.

\_\_\_\_ Acknowledge and understand school norms and related traditions.

____ Recognize and value essential facets of all learning community members.
____ Appreciate and incorporate school district policies, regulations, and procedures.

Impressed, Superintendent Boulle recommended that his associate superintendent immediately begin initiating a plan for implementation, first collaborating with other members of the administrative cabinet and involving their ideas and suggestions, and then bring a proposal to his office within the next two weeks.

## Pause and Consider

1. What do you perceive to be the essential, if not critical, expectations of the new principal role? How do position responsibilities differ from role expectations? Explain.
2. What are the institutional norms in your school? Can you identify certain campus traditions? Do you believe the noted norms and traditions enhance or interfere with teaching, leading, and learning? Justify your response.
3. What aspects essential to school leadership must a new principal recognize and learn as related to the learning community at large? Who makes up the learning community of a school, and which members of the learning community are most critical to a new principal's success? Least critical? Expound upon your answers.
4. Why must a new principal be familiar with school district policies, regulations, and/or procedures? Describe how such a familiarization process predicates success for a new principal.

## THE NEW PRINCIPAL—YESTERYEAR AND TODAY: HAS ANYTHING CHANGED BUT THE DATE ON THE CALENDAR?

What were the functions of the new principalship at least five decades ago compared to those of new principals today? First, as a means of establishing a baseline, new principals of the late 1960s and throughout the 1970s, even into the 1990s, were largely male (80 percent or more) and devoted approximately forty to forty-five hours per week to the role and position (Babcock, 1991; Helterbran & Rieg, 2004; Zippa, 2022a), typically leaving the office close to 5:00 p.m. daily. Today, new school leaders are exceedingly female

(55 percent) and dedicate approximately sixty to eighty hours per week to the profession (National Council for Education Statistics [NCES], 2020).

Second, student management (disciplinary issues) and building maintenance and operations were time-consuming functions of the new principals of yesteryear, followed by extracurricular activities and scheduling—the latter often delegated to campus registrars (McPeake, 2007). Today, new principals continue to allocate a vast amount of their time to school management activities and personnel but are now expected to focus on program development, professional development, and instructionally oriented meetings.

Third, new principals today must not only ensure student achievement but also maintain a positive school climate and open culture, motivate personnel, and enhance effective teaching and learning practices (Levin & Bradley, 2019). Today, however, new principals devote significantly less time, as noted in the studies previously sourced, to student behavior and discipline, student activities, and office work.

Fourth, new principals of years past were profiled as (1) being White males approximately fifty years of age; (2) working, on average, an eight-hour day; (3) having good morals; and (4) spending a good portion of an instructional day disciplining students and supervising staff. Certainly, new principals of yesteryear were engaged in a "man's educational work world," developing relationships with male administrative colleagues and a largely female faculty and staff. Have such attributes changed as far as today's new principals are concerned? Absolutely—with a few caveats!

Today, as was the case from 1960 to 1990, the typical new principal is slightly less than fifty years old (forty-six years of age), and mostly White (68 percent). Not reasonable and definitely discriminatory, the following statistic is, sadly, no different today than in the past: Ninety-four percent of female principals earn less than their male counterparts (NCES, 2020). That noted, it must be emphasized that women today are defining, if not redefining—for the better—the role of the new principalship. Just as important, women are reshaping and recharacterizing their own personal relationships while interacting with male administrative colleagues. Finally, as was true in years past, female principals continue to work with predominately female teaching staffs.

What is known today: Fifteen percent of new principals are self-identified as LGBTQ+. How different the LGBTQ+ profile of yesteryear varies from new principals today is relatively unknown, but it is readily acknowledged that self-identifying as LGBTQ+ in the late 1960s into the 1990s—that is, coming out to others—was at the very least extremely difficult and certainly job threatening (Hall, Dawes & Plocek, 2021; Zippa, 2022a).

New principals today are expected to aid students who are not performing to potential, as well as personally lead professional development and also manage the financial resources (budget) of a school. Today, new principals are expected to attract quality teachers and recruit professionals (assistant principals) who eventually will either replace the school leader or other district K–12 principals.

Today's new principals are presumed, if not required, to work with social service agencies; interact positively and cooperatively with parents; collaboratively engage and network with faculty relative to site-based decision-making; develop and renew curriculum; conduct research and/or examine the research literature; create and foster new student-centered instructional practices; and ensure that district, state, and federal accountability standards are met and further exceed expectations year after year. Today the new principalship has been described as a ten-thousand-aspirin job! If such is a relevant descriptor, what are the essential new principal attributes to becoming a successful school leader?

## NEW PRINCIPAL EXPECTATIONS, SKILL SETS, AND ATTRIBUTES: A TALE OF THEN AND NOW

Then, new principals typically kept the boat afloat and, moreover, ensured that they did not rock the boat. In other words, the new principals of yesteryear could best be described as bosses, supervisors, superiors, and most certainly managers. New principals then advanced a theory of compliance—not only for themselves but also for faculty, students, and parents and, undoubtedly, for career longevity. The principalship, new or tenured in those days, was different. Examine the offered scenario and respond to the Pause and Consider queries that follow.

### I'M A COUPLE OF GENERATIONS TOO LATE!

Eddie Anderson sat in his office after another lengthy day at Benjamin Kubelsky School. Anderson, the school's new principal, was in his first year of administrative service and was simply worn out that late-fall afternoon. His mentor, university professor Dr. Celeste Skyler, unexpectedly walked in and said, "Hello, Eddie, what are you doing? I bet you are sitting there thinking great thoughts!" Eddie laughed and warmly welcomed Dr. Skyler.

Dr. Skyler asked how Eddie's first semester as school leader was proceeding. New principal Anderson responded with a sigh and raised eyebrows, revealing just how challenging his role as school leader had been. "Tell me about it, Eddie," Dr. Skyler prodded. Anderson responded by stating, "This isn't what I had expected, and it certainly isn't what I trained for during either my principal preparation program or my assistant principalship!"

Anderson went on to share: "The expectations as a new principal are sky-high. The position requires a very explicit and detailed set of skills and personal characteristics along with specific leadership attributes—many of which were never mentioned during my recruiting process. I often think that I'm a couple of generations too late to the principalship."

Dr. Skyler nodded empathetically. The professor of long tenure at Union State of the Southwest University shared how she recalled the principalship of yesteryear, back in the late 1960s and early 1970s, when she began her career in education as a teacher. Dr. Skyler prefaced her account by saying that what she was about to share was not intended to minimize or maximize the principal role and expectations of today. She simply acknowledged that today's principalship was very different, and for good reason, compared to the principalship of the past.

"Eddie, back in the day, I vividly recall my first principal—a tough-skinned World War II veteran—who said successful principals followed the 3 Bs of administrative leadership: Books, Buses, and Butts! In those days, principals managed. They managed the distribution of textbooks, managed the morning unloading and afternoon loading of school buses, and managed student discipline by means of corporal punishment.

"Yes, Eddie, a couple of generations back, leading as a school principal was quite different. I'm not saying it was easier back then, as I suspect you are thinking. What I am trying to relate is the fact that I'm not certain—actually, I don't believe—those principals of yesteryear could readily and effectively sit in your chair and serve as instructional leaders today."

Dr. Skyler then genuinely revealed how she would like to learn more about the new principal role so that improvement could be made relative to the university principal preparation program. At that point, new principal Anderson began a revealing explanation and discussion of required and current new principal expectations, associated skills sets, and five attributes that best ensured administrative success.

## Pause and Consider

1. Identify what you perceive to be the "now, the current" new principal expectations essential for administrative success.
2. Prepare and share a list of special skill sets necessary for a new principal to flourish in the administrative role.
3. What are new principal attributes (features, elements of leadership) critical to being a competent school leader? Explain why.
4. Which of the self-identified expectations, skill sets, and principal attributes are being presented in your principal preparation program or school district new principal mentoring program? Which are not and definitely should be? Read on for further information and clarification.

## The Attributes: A Brief Introduction

As previously advanced in the "Happenstance It Is Not!" textbox scenario, this chapter concludes with a brief introduction to the five critical attributes required to become a successful new principal. Each of the five attributes will be expounded upon within subsequent chapters.

New principals must:

1. ***Learn the role expectations and accept position responsibilities.***

    Each school year thousands of new principals begin a career opportunity that can and will be challenging, often frustrating, and exhausting, yet also stimulating, interesting, thought-provoking, inspiring, and amazingly rewarding. Routines will be few, as every day is a new day filled with new and different perplexing and demanding tasks that can readily tax the mind. Be aware that this list of descriptors has yet to identify all the potential complaints that must be met with a smile, a listening ear, an open mind, and/or a resolve to please, if not placate, all parties.

    What are the expectations and responsibilities associated with the new principal role? Identified below is a list of what is expected of the new school leader and, just as important, responsibilities of a new principal.

    __ Listen to stakeholders.
    __ Be visible and maintain an open-door policy.
    __ Interact with students and teachers during instruction time.
    __ Control the narrative.
    __ Talk the talk, but be certain to walk the walk.
    __ Transition into the new role and learn to surmount a significant learning curve.

___ Establish relationships.
___ Learn the culture and enhance the climate.
___ Respect the faculty and staff.
___ Choose each battle carefully.
___ Delegate: Never dump!
___ Plan on a lasting career and eventual legacy.
___ Get to know supervisors and interact with these individuals regularly.
___ Understand who is a team player and who is not.
___ Be organized and focus on the details.

2. *Acquire and possess essential if not critical skills, traits, and characteristics.*

   In their classic text *Leadership: Enhancing the Lessons of Experience*, tenth edition (2021), Hughes, Ginnett, and Curphy remind new principals that leaders are made, not born. Leaders being born and not made is nothing more than a myth. Recognize that individuals grow best as leaders when faced with adversities, challenges, and the forge of experiences. However, a most important question deserving of an answer: What are the critical skills, traits, and characteristics that must be acquired and continuously possessed? Sorenson and Goldsmith (2009) and Northouse (2021) share specific characteristics and traits new principals must possess. For example, new principals must be:

   ___ Self-confident
   ___ Dependable
   ___ Energetic
   ___ Intelligent
   ___ Tolerant
   ___ Flexible and adjustable
   ___ Sociable
   ___ Even-tempered
   ___ Assertive
   ___ Visionary
   ___ Ethical, with moral values
   ___ Quality-orientated
   ___ Communicative (to include being an active listener)
   ___ Firm, fair, and friendly: the 3 Fs of effective new principal leadership

3. *Acknowledge and understand school norms and related traditions.*

   The term "norms" typically refers to some aspect of schooling that is usual, standard, expected, mainstream, conventional, or, simply put, normal. Norms refer to certain and often established behaviors, attitudes, and values that are consistent with members of the learning community and society. There are generally four types of norms within society and thus within the micro-society called school. These are folkways (common habits, traditions, and/or customs), mores (ethics, morals, and/or standards), taboos (prohibitions, restrictions, and/or orders), and laws (policies, regulations, and/or rules).

Following are a few basic examples for new principals to observe:
- __ Acknowledge others in passing.
- __ Meet and greet students and parents.
- __ Incorporate a warm and welcoming attitude and exhibit a sense of humor when appropriate.
- __ Be a team member and serve as the team leader.
- __ Collaborate with all members of the learning community.
- __ Follow board policies.
- __ Recognize established campus rules and regulations.
- __ Be instructionally focused and student-centered.
- __ Exert strong ethical and moral convictions.
- __ Avoid inappropriate behaviors (sexual, physical, and/or emotional actions such as sexual harassment, being disrespectful of others, bullying, yelling, exhibiting excessive control and/or micromanaging, disregarding duties and responsibilities, insubordination, and—definitely—condoning violence).
- __ Know, incorporate, and attend certain campus traditions such as awards ceremonies, open houses, parent-teacher organization meetings, and student-oriented and/or extracurricular activities.

The topic of norms and traditions, as well as customs, will be explored in greater detail in chapter 6, "Step # 4: Acknowledge and Understand School Norms, Traditions, and Customs."

4. *Recognize and value essential facets of all learning community members.*

New principals must know, understand, and value the cultures, customs, and expectations of community members—both within and beyond the school setting. Essential facets include but are not limited to equality, equity, and empathy, as well as honoring the home language of students, parents, other community members, and business and religious leaders.

Other essential facets critical to a new principal's success include recognizing that much can be learned, shared, and integrated within and across the learning community. New school leaders must understand the principled beliefs and lifestyles of others, which may seem different or unusual. Such facets are not only what develop and enhance cultures but also bring campus dynamics to life, bring people together, and are certainly worthy of recognition and celebration.

Games and leisure activities of learning community members create opportunities for establishing meaningful relationships. Also consider that certain community member holidays, clothing, hairstyles, rituals, and languages not necessarily common to a school principal or faculty and staff are important to recognize and incorporate into the campus curriculum, instructional program, and other campus activities.

Carefully consider and grasp the significance of the words of Tony Hsieh (American internet entrepreneur) and then Amy Poehler (American comedian, actress, writer, producer, and director): "If you get the culture right, most of the other stuff will just take care of itself" (Tony Hsieh, GoogleQuotes.com, 2022b), and "Find a group of people who challenge and inspire you, spend a lot of time with them, and it will change your life forever" (Amy Poehler, GoogleQuotes.com, 2022b).

Valuing essential facets of the learning community fosters growth, which leads to further exploration, ultimately yielding inspiration and increasing the curiosity, passion, and purpose of both students and families. Valuing essential facets of a learning community is crucial. It is the root of all academic, personal, and social momentum. Valuing community is a means of distributive leadership, thus offering a wide range of leadership roles, skill-building opportunities, and an acceleration of impactful relationships, all of which serve to increase student achievement and success in life.

5. *Appreciate, incorporate, and obey school district policies, regulations, and procedures.*

    School board or district policies are statements of decisions, principles, or courses of action related to the guidance and governance of a school system and are frequently based on the legal application of education code and/or court rulings. Administrative regulations are statements as to how board policy is to be applied and implemented by a school district's administrative team. Campus procedures are those written statements or sometimes unwritten expectations applied, most notably to personnel. An example: "Be certain to check out at the office if leaving campus during a conference or planning period."

    Remember, on any given day a new principal is faced with a barrage of issues and problems that require following board policies, district regulations, or campus procedures. To overlook or ignore such is to endanger not only self but all members of the learning community. School district board policies, administrative regulations, and campus procedures are "helping-hands" or "lifelines" designed to ensure that a new principal avoids legal entanglements. In the forthcoming chapters, each of the five attributes will be further explored.

## FINAL THOUGHTS

The new principals of yesteryear were mostly responsible for keeping the proverbial "boat afloat" and certainly not "rocking the boat." In other words, the new principals of decades ago engaged in managerial absolutes such as focusing on administrative functions (commonly referred to as the 3 Bs: Books, Buses, and Butts). These new principals took care of the distribution and retrieval of textbooks, organized the bookroom, monitored the loading and unloading of students from buses, and, of course, handled student disciplinary issues.

The new principals of yesteryear were responsible for managing personnel (hiring, retaining, and dismissal of teachers), maintaining campus operations, managing the budget, supervising teachers and staff, as well as student and teacher scheduling and managing those emergent social forces that related mostly to extending educational opportunities, especially in an era of civil and equal rights. The question always worthy of consideration: The new principals of yesteryear and those of today—has anything changed but the date on the calendar?

To initially answer that question, first a baseline must be established. Who were the new principals of years past in comparison to the new principals of today? Second, what were the new principal managerial tasks of yesteryear relative to those of new principals today? Third, to what degree were new principals of decades ago responsible for instructional leadership when compared with today's new principals? Fourth, a comparative profiling of new principals of the past and those of today is worthy of contemplation. Lastly, new principal expectations—a tale of then and now—are warranted relative to identified skill sets and essential attributes.

Finally, this first chapter briefly introduced those critical attributes for new principal success today: (1) Learn the role expectations and accept position responsibilities; (2) acquire and possess essential if not critical skills, traits, and characteristics; (3) acknowledge and understand school norms and related traditions; (4) recognize and value essential facets of all learning community members; and (5) appreciate, incorporate, and obey school district policies, administrative regulations, and campus procedures. As a reminder, each of the five attributes will be further examined and detailed in chapters to come.

## DISCUSSION QUESTIONS

1. Identify the expectations of new principals of decades past and compare them with the new principals of today. In your estimation, which of the differences are most glaring? Explain.

2. New principals of yesteryear and those of today: Has anything changed but the date on the calendar? Be detailed and enlightening in your response.
3. Develop a baseline or profile of new principals of years past relative to those of today. Was new principal Eddie Anderson correct (in the chapter textbox) regarding his summation: "I'm a couple of generations too late!" Yes or no? How or why?
4. Examine the five attributes essential to new principal success and explain which one of the five is most critical to administrative achievement. Expand upon your answer.

## CASE STUDY APPLICATION: HOW ARE OUR NEW SCHOOL LEADERS DOING, LIZ?

Dr. Nina McKinney, superintendent of the Granby Acres School District, was determined to get out of her office this early fall morning and travel to Katy Cypress School to visit a new principal, Nataly Morales, and her assistant principal, Ryan Paulson. Both Nataly and Ryan were new school leaders, an unusual pairing, as both had limited administrative experience. Nataly had previously served for two years as an assistant principal in another school district; Ryan was an inexperienced assistant principal. Both Nataly and Ryan had strong educational credentials, however, and were thus selected for their competence as educators and their outstanding résumés and previous professional accomplishments.

Entering Katy Cypress's office, Dr. McKinney was warmly greeted by the campus secretary, Liz Cooper. Ms. Cooper had worked for several years as secretary for the campus and had served with the previous three long-term and beloved school principals, Ruth Perrot, Iris Atterbury, and Frank Fontaine. She now was present to aid the new school principal, Nataly Morales, and her assistant, Ryan Paulson, in any way possible. Immediately, a conversation ensued:

*Liz Cooper*   Good morning, Dr. McKinney! So glad to see you!

*Dr. Nina McKinney*   Well, hello, and how is the school secretary today? And, by the way, how are our new school leaders doing, Liz?

*Liz Cooper*   I'm fine, Dr. McKinney, and they are doing well. I think they actually have a surprisingly good handle on their tasks at hand. Of course, as you well know, time will tell. Excuse me; I'll let Nataly and Ryan know you are here to see them.

*Dr. McKinney*   Thank you, Liz. Have a wonderful day!

Dr. McKinney walked down the office hallway and was greeted with hand extended by Nataly Morales, the new principal at Katy Cypress School. The two made their way into Nataly's office and were soon joined by Assistant Principal Ryan Paulson. After the initial greetings, the superintendent of schools began an inquisitive conversation:

> ***Dr. McKinney*** I'm glad to see that you two are settling in. I'm already hearing good things about your leadership approach here at Katy Cypress. I'd like to ask a few questions and receive some feedback from both of you.
>
> ***Nataly Morales*** Yes, Dr. McKinney, please do. Fortunately, Ryan and I have both returned from visiting classrooms and interacting with a team of teachers. Earlier today, we both sat in on the parent-teacher organization executive committee meeting. Our new parent-teacher president is Laverne Shirley, a wonderful and insightful parent who is helping us fund additional library books.
>
> ***Dr. McKinney*** Glad to hear it, Nataly. Now, if I may, let's get to the heart of my visit. Let me pose a question or two: Tell me, what are you two doing relative to my recommendation that each of you develop a personal plan of action?
>
> ***Nataly Morales*** Both Ryan and I have worked hard, mostly after school hours, as our days are filled with numerous other responsibilities. First, we have identified what we believe are critical skills essential for our success as school leaders. Second, we are developing a plan of action that will guide us as we focus on what new educational leaders must do for success. Third, we have enlisted the support of retired principal Xavier Barrera, who has graciously agreed to serve as our mentor.
>
> ***Dr. McKinney*** That is good news, folks! I have great faith in Xavier and consider him an exceptional school leader and an amazing human being. You two are fortunate to have acquired his services.
>
> ***Ryan Paulson*** We couldn't agree more! Mr. Barrera, for starters, has helped us in overcoming new principal isolation. As our mentor, he is guiding us as we develop our personal plan but also as we contemplate a critical framework for success.
>
> ***Nataly Morales*** Also, Dr. McKinney, we are developing a networking support process with a few of our district colleagues, Dr. Lloyd Goldsmith, Teresa Cortez, Barbara McIntyre, and Cindy Clendennen, all of whom have been helpful in guiding us as we begin to initiate the research of Paul Bambrick-Santoyo and Doug Lemov and implement their instructional models.
>
> ***Dr. McKinney*** I'm impressed. Good work! Questions either of you have for me?

Both Principal Morales and Assistant Principal Paulson had several questions, which they posed to the superintendent. Following the question-and-answer session, Nataly and Ryan did a brief tour of the campus with Dr. McKinney, who soon excused herself and made a dash to visit another nearby campus.

## Application Questions

1. What aspects of the chapter's new principal attributes are the focus of the conversation between new principal Nataly Morales, new assistant principal Ryan Paulson, and the superintendent of schools? Recognize that both the principal and assistant principal are new in their roles. Which of the new principal attributes might prove most beneficial to this "newly formed" administrative team?
2. Carefully examine the conversation between the new school leaders and the superintendent and share why enlisting the support of a retired principal, Xavier Barrera, could best benefit the new principal and her assistant principal. Provide a detailed analysis.
3. What is the benefit of the new school leaders having a mentor as well as interacting with the four noted school district administrative colleagues? Explain why.
4. What might be included in a new principal's personal plan and/or critical framework for success? Provide a brief list of examples.
5. One interesting tidbit noted early in the case study conversation is that of the interaction between Dr. Nina McKinney, superintendent of schools, and Liz Cooper, Katy Cypress School secretary. What are the benefits of a long-term secretary to a new principal? Perceived detriments? Rationalize your answers.

*Chapter 2*

# Step #1: Advance Critical New Principal Skills

## *Develop a Plan for Success*

> The only thing tougher than developing leadership skills is attempting to be successful without them.
> (Orrin Woodward, *New York Times* bestselling author, AZQuotes.com, 2022c)

**DEVELOPING A PLAN OF ACTION FOR SUCCESS**

New principals have one thing on their mind with the start of school: "How do I survive?" Good question with a quick if not condescending answer once revealed by another new principal: "Don't screw up!" Well, true, but that response does little to alleviate the concerns of principals new to the field of school leadership. The flippant answer provides little to no guidance. So, how does a new principal succeed without failing? Before the start of the school year, develop a plan of action for leadership success.

A new principal's plan of action must be predicated by and grounded in the research literature, and as noted in Step #1: Advance Critical New Principal Skills. What do decades of principal leadership research reveal? Specifically, when it comes to surviving the first year—the year every principal experienced and endured and yet, chances are, survived. Consider the following:

1. Identify personal leadership strengths, and focus on and target those areas for personal leadership growth and development.
2. Establish a timeline by which strengths will be better honed and targeted areas will be enhanced or improved.

3. Pinpoint specific techniques, methods, strategies, actions, and/or activities that will guide in the skill development and improvement process.

Listed below are a few new principal leadership considerations and examples that can prove helpful in developing, for legitimate success, a personal plan of action.

1. Identify and incorporate specific leadership skills already possessed, and address and advance those critical skills that must be gained and mastered.
   Examples:
   - *Commit to a clear plan of action and a doable vision.* Determine what needs to be accomplished today, tomorrow, this week, this month, this semester, this year, next year, and so forth. Jot down (hard copy or digital) the visionary commitments. Devote yourself to a one- to three-year plan. Adjustments will occur, often immediately. That is okay. Keep moving forward with eyes on the prize!
   - *Prioritize leadership skills necessary to put into practice as part of the action and visionary plan.* Determine what key skills will aid in successful leadership performance. Again, know your strengths and be aware of areas to target for personal and professional growth and development.
   - *Collaborate and coordinate with members of the leadership team and teaching teams.* The absolute best principals collaborate (I'm here to work with you), facilitate (I'm here to help you), and coordinate (I'm here to organize, systemize, and maximize with you). Join in and work cooperatively to achieve the action and visionary plan, always focusing on student achievement and organizational success.
   - *Entrust tasks and responsibilities to team members, always monitoring the process.* Recall the old Russian proverb: "*Doveryai, no provergai,*" meaning "Trust but verify." Delegate (never dump) tasks and assignments. However, inspect what is expected. Trust, ownership, and followership will ensue as a result. This is effective leadership!
   - *Establish high expectations and standards.* High expectations promote achievement orientation, self-esteem in others, and feelings of self-efficacy, motivation, and well-being.
   - *Serve as an honorable, ethical, moral, and hardworking role model.* Be credible, provide earnest and responsible direction, and practice what is preached.
   - *ALWAYS pursue guidance and advice.* Always seek the guidance of master teachers, supervisors, colleagues, and, most certainly, mentors.

- *Know and understand personalities.* Conflicts will arise early. Be proactive. Recognize trouble before trouble begins. People are people. Some are headstrong, others sensitive. Some are passive, others aggressive. Some, it must be noted, are simply resisters. For a better perspective, read the brief but informative *Responding to Resisters: Tactics That Work for Principals* (Sorenson, 2021).
2. Recognize specific decision-making and problem-solving skills to be possessed. Examples:
   - *Analyze data before making instructional decisions.* Data-based decision-making best ensures that academic-related commitments are research-based, student-centered, and best practice–oriented.
   - *Be creative, think imaginatively, and take risks. However, always use good judgment and sound common sense.* New principals deserve some leeway. A mistake can be made. A failure can occur. Ensure that all aspects of creative risk are conducted with the best of intentions. If failure occurs, chances are that supervisors, teachers, and parents will be forgiving, at least this one time. After that, consider the honeymoon over!
3. Isolate and enhance specific communication skills essential to new principal success.
   Example:
   - *Sound and effective communication is a key skill to success.* A new principal must emulate the most essential communication behaviors (the 12 Bs):
   - *Be frequent, be proactive, be honest, be prepared, be collaborative, be networking, be online and engaged in social media, be humorous, be appreciative, be empathetic, be clear and concise, and always be truthful.*
4. Pinpoint specific self-management skills necessary for success.
   Example:
   - *Manage time and organization skills, manage pressure, manage deadlines, manage personal as well as professional goals, and manage self by incorporating personal skill sets and setting an exceptional example.*
5. Ascertain specific personal attributes crucial to being an effective school leader. For example, see the next section, "Critical Leader Skills Identified: What's a New Principal to Do?"

Finally, incorporate and utilize each of the above-noted planning measures and calculated skills and actions as a means of reflective practice and assessment relative to new leadership capabilities. Create a personal plan for professional growth and development. Identify specific actions to be initiated and completed. As part of the plan, incorporate Step #1 and advance critical new principal skills as a means of establishing and maintaining a timeline for success.

## CRITICAL LEADER SKILLS IDENTIFIED: WHAT'S A NEW PRINCIPAL TO DO?

Orrin Woodward, in the opening quote, is absolutely correct! The last thing a new principal should ever attempt to do is be successful without possessing essential leadership skills when leading and guiding a learning community. A question to pose beyond "What's a new principal to do?" is "What critical leadership skills must a new principal acquire and continuously develop?" Previously noted in chapter 1 was a sample list of essential new principal skills. For the purpose of review and further expansion, below is a list of skills crucial to leader success. New principals must be:

- __ Self-confident
- __ Dependable
- __ Energetic
- __ Intelligent
- __ Tolerant
- __ Empowering
- __ Collaborative
- __ Facilitative
- __ Humorous
- __ Direct
- __ Communicative
- __ Creative (risk-taking)
- __ Trustworthy
- __ Encouraging
- __ Responsible
- __ Organized
- __ Social
- __ Supportive
- __ Motivated
- __ Perceptive
- __ Assertive
- __ Visionary
- __ Even-tempered
- __ Goal-driven

__ Active listener
__ Decision-maker
__ Problem-solver
__ Student-centered
__ Quality-focused
__ Performance-driven
__ Achievement-oriented
__ Honest and truthful
__ Flexible and adjustable
__ Ethical, with moral values

Obviously, this is quite a laundry list of skills, traits, characteristics, and attributes. Two important questions now arise relative to skill acquisition and development. Question #1: Is it doable or attainable for a new principal to gain the identified essential skills? Question #2: How and by what means does a new principal gain all of the noted skills? Consider the next section.

## PRACTICAL PERSPECTIVES FOR NEW PRINCIPALS: SKILLS ACQUISITION

From a practical perspective, as realized in Step #1: Advance Critical New Principal Skills, unexperienced principals must identify, acquire, develop, demonstrate, and master a menagerie of leadership skills. Easy? Not necessarily! Possible? Absolutely! How and by what means can a new principal gain the above-noted listing?

New principals must learn how to (1) assess faculty and staff, (2) conduct group meetings, (3) identify goals and objectives for leading, (4) reveal a penchant for outstanding teaching and essential learning, (5) design and implement a campus improvement plan, (6) engage in data-based decision-making and problem-solving processes, (7) collaborate and facilitate, (8) align curriculum with instruction, (9) read the research literature, and finally (10) incorporate best instructional practices. Once again, quite a laundry list!

Furthermore, a new principal must be change-oriented; demonstrate self-awareness; exhibit discernment; develop and manage a school budget; effectively utilize time-management skills; understand educational laws and school board policies; establish leadership authority; manage school personnel; develop professional relationships; interact with students, parents, and community members as well as district professional staff and supervisors; and readily recognize and stay within a multitude of professional parameters. That laundry list continues to grow!

The new principal must network within the school and beyond the campus building, developing positive working relationships inside the school organizations (e.g., parent-teacher) and with outside agencies (e.g., Child Protective Services, social services, physical and mental health services, and community and/or district police). The laundry list continues to expand!

Finally, the new principal must recognize and utilize the previously identified personal leadership skills, traits, characteristics, and talents and work to improve personal areas targeted for professional growth and development; develop a personal plan of action; nurture a framework for leadership success; and, most important of all, be seriously and significantly student-centered. As one new principal put it, "It's a tough row to hoe!" The laundry list definitely presents a new principal with a steep learning curve!

Some would say there is no curve at all because, simply put, there is a straight and narrow line that goes from the first day on the job to an almost immediate development and acquisition of those learned and essential skills! Which brings up another question: "Are you certain you want to be a school principal?" Do not close this book! You have worked too hard to reach this point in your career. Respond in the affirmative because you have the intrinsic motivation, tenacity, perseverance, and determination to succeed! Believe it or not, it is all possible and achievable. Read on!

## How to Gain the Required New Principal Leadership Skills

Leading is not easy. No one ever said it would be. For a new principal to think so is the quickest way to leadership failure. Examine the fifteen "how and by what means" listings, and understand how new principal leadership skills can be acquired:

1. *Practice self-discipline* (a new principal being able to control their personal feelings). Self-discipline is having the potential to overcome any personal weaknesses—the ability to pursue what is appropriate and justified despite desires, appeals, persuasions, or enticements to abandon what is applicable and proper.
2. *Seek additional leadership roles and responsibilities*, first as a teacher and, most certainly, as an assistant principal. Early on-the-job training prior to a principalship is always most beneficial.
3. *Lead, but also recognize the "collective we"* as a skillful method of learning to lead. Incorporated by a new principal, the "collective we" orientation is the process of attaining individual goals by participating in group efforts designed to ensure organizational success. From a school leadership perspective, the "collective we" is overcoming

the "individual I" by managing ego, being loyal to the team, exhibiting humility, demonstrating a strong work ethic, displaying courage, being an active listener seeking sound advice, utilizing tactfulness, and unveiling a teamwork orientation.

Leading as a member of the "collective we" is all about delegating (remember, *not* dumping) and sharing responsibilities which can contribute to a positive instructional team culture of support and respect. When a new principal is willing to include followers on certain projects, others then have an opportunity to lead and grow as a team. New principals who engage in the "collective we" as a leadership model invest in group efforts, advance the quality of student-oriented projects, and, ultimately, drive team and organizational improvements.

4. *Develop situational awareness.* A new principal is acutely aware of what is occurring relative to where they are, where they are supposed to be, and whether anyone or anything around the new principal is a threat to the overall success of the leader and/or the learning community.
5. *Incorporate situational leadership as a leader style.* Situational leadership for the new principal simply means adapting leadership skills to the situation or task that best meets the needs of a team member or the entire team. Ken Blanchard and Paul Hersey developed the Situational Leadership Theory in 1969, as they strongly believed there was no "one size fits all" form of leadership (Yukl & Gardner, 2019). This specific leadership skill was based on recognizing the situation at hand. Incorporating situational leadership is all about diagnosing the situation, applying flexibility in responding to the situation, and then solving or resolving the situation with the appropriate leadership skill or skills.

    Situational leadership is all about utilizing differing skills at the time, being aware of how to best approach a situation, and aiding faculty in working out issues. Additionally, situational leadership frequently boosts leader performance when addressing a problem, as opposed to utilizing an autocratic or authoritative approach, which can not only be heavy-handed but often unnecessary.

    For example, a new principal can incorporate a democratic or even a transactional approach to working through problematic issues; as a result, all parties may very well walk away realizing that the situation at hand has been effectively resolved. Moreover, all parties are apt to feel positive about the circumstance and the resolution and even enlightened, being more open-minded and informed as to how to solve such an issue or problem in the future.
6. *Be inspirational.* Examine the leading efforts of outstanding athletic coaches. These women and men are rousing, encouraging, and motivating. Inspirational principals are value-driven, purposeful, and

responsible; create positive change; provide passion; and listen with a meaningful purpose. They act, they overcome, and they are innovative and forward-thinking. Consider this adage related to inspiring leadership: "If I persist, I continue to try. If I try, I continue to move forward. If I move forward, I succeed."

7. *Serve as the lead learner*. New principals who are lead learners are always reading, researching, attending professional development meetings, and leading on-campus in-service sessions. These principals lead to learn and learn to lead.
8. *Recognize conflict before it evolves*. New principals must be immediately prepared to resolve conflict. New principals who are proactive are focused on preparation. New principals who are reactive are, regrettably, focused on restoration.
9. *Learn by listening*. Active listening is a method of listening to learn. The new principal responds to another individual's statement by saying, "Based on what I heard, you inferred . . ." This mode of listening better ensures mutual understanding.
10. *Engage in educational conferences and professional development* where effective leadership programs are available. New principals are wise to participate in learning opportunities relative to gaining essential leadership skills.
11. *Establish personal goals to become professionally adept and successful*. Setting goals brings about new and better leadership behaviors, guides personal and professional focus, and helps sustain a sense of measurement and self-mastery, both important to individual and organizational success.
12. *Network with other principals*. Develop a strong and lasting relationship with a mentor. Networking allows a new principal to develop district partners as well as professional acquaintances. Networking better enables skill development and career path progression and is a powerful tool for making friends and overcoming reticent, timid, or reserved behaviors.
13. *Master "soft" skills*. These are personal attributes that enable a new principal to interact effectively and harmoniously with members of the learning community. Soft skill examples are communication, teamwork, problem-solving, critical thinking, decision-making, stress management, and, most essential, personality and relationship traits and behaviors.
14. *Understand and utilize, as appropriate, primary leadership styles*. Examples are situational, transformational, transactional, servant, democratic, democratic-manipulation, autocratic, authoritative, bureaucratic, laissez-faire, and charismatic.
15. *Ask for help—ALWAYS!*

***Note:*** Fortune 500 and Korn Ferry each year collaborate to identify the World's Most Admired Companies as a means of examining how highly regarded and successful firms are most prominent and what makes these firms stand out from a leadership skills perspective (Royal & Manson-Smith, 2023). This process involves more than six hundred firms and a survey of more than thirty-seven hundred executive leaders.

Most applicable to school systems and, more specifically, to both tenured and new principals is the following postpandemic data and information: (1) Talent acquisition is the one area these top organizations are most focused, (2) developing individuals for new workplace challenges and/or different work is priority one, (3) committing additional resources to new skills acquisition is critical, (4) conducting annual strategic workforce planning is an added benefit; and (5) motivating existing employees to enhance skill development to better assist with sustainable initiatives is essential.

New principals must be attuned to and give serious consideration to the noted applications relative to skills enhancement and acquisition in terms of faculty and staff. Much can be learned from the Fortune 500 companies and their leaders.

## KEYS TO PERSONAL GROWTH AND DEVELOPMENT

Personal growth and development for any new principal wishing to maximize the leadership role and skill acquisition must be a lifelong goal and journey. Enriching life and career through self-evolvement, improvement, and advancement augments the building of enhanced skills, better relationships, and a more satisfying career. Identified below are seven keys (also known as skills) to a new principal's personal as well as professional advancement and success as proposed by Ramanathan (2019) and Sorenson, Goldsmith, and DeMatthews (2016):

1. *Be the lead learner and apply new learning.* Possessing an instinctive drive to learn and then apply any gained knowledge and skill enhancement will have a positive impact on personal and professional growth and development. Keeping up with the latest in educational research and instructional trends ensures positive in-school ramifications. Learning and developing strengths, talents, and abilities not only expands knowledge but better ensures personal success, student achievement, teacher advancement, and, of course, career longevity.
2. *Take risks.* Chancing possibilities is more than a gamble; it is a risk worth taking. Risk-takers are much more apt to gain success. Recall

three leadership and risk-oriented quotes: "If you want some ham, you gotta go into the smokehouse" (Huey Long); "He who would eat the fruit must climb the tree" (old Scottish proverb); and "Failure is not the opposite of success. Failure as a result of risk is a part of success" (Anonymous) (Vamboa.org, 2022).
3. *Reflect and self-evaluate.* Self-awareness, as previously noted, is essential to a new principal. Self-evaluation provides an opportunity to reflect on and respond to four central questions: (a) What is life and profession like now? (b) What is desired in life and career in the future that is not apparent today? (c) What is required to make essential change? (d) What timeline or goal-setting process to success needs to be established? See the self-evaluative instrument in chapter 9.
4. *Time management is important.* Sorenson, Goldsmith, and DeMatthews (2016) remind new principals that time management is at the heart of school leadership. Learn to utilize time both effectively and beneficially. And remember this: Forget the time lost, appreciate the time that remains, and look forward to making the best of the time that is forthcoming. Recognize this also: Time is fleeting—capture it and use it to benefit self and the learning community!
5. *Organization is essential.* New principals must learn to set boundaries, both professional and personal. The best leaders are organized. They prioritize; increase visibility; distribute leadership; set goals; utilize an agenda; create to-do lists; limit distractions; practice accountability; maintain a clear, clean, and uncluttered desk and office environment; clearly label and file (both hard copy and electronically) paperwork; and sort emails multiple times each day. An exceptional read relative to the noted topics and to time management is *The Principal's Guide to Time Management: Instructional Leadership in the Digital Age* (2016).
6. *Take care of self.* A new principal's development and health are both readily achieved when five growth factors are acknowledged and initiated:
    - *Mental growth.* Focus on how to reflect and learn effectively and efficiently. Seek district-based or private mental and emotional health therapy. Seeing a therapist is no longer taboo. Taking care of self is often a necessity for life and career improvement and enhancement, if not survival. Therapeutic counseling works!
    - *Social growth.* Improve communication skills—enunciate clearly, speak up so all can hear and learn, and actively listen. Intermingle and interact with all members of the learning community.
    - *Spiritual growth.* Practice prayer or regularly meditate to manage stress and build confidence.

- *Emotional growth.* Develop and manage personal well-being to overcome challenges, stress, and anxieties.
- *Physical growth.* Exercise regularly, eat healthy, and ensure adequate sleep. Each of these physically oriented activities is an essential key to not only stamina but also well-being in the new principalship.

   For new principals desiring an associated read, turn to *Equity, Equality, and Empathy: What Principals Can Do for the Well-Being of the Learning Community* (Sorenson, 2022).
7. *Find a mentor.* Previously noted and worth repeating, it is very important to identify, confide in, and utilize an individual who can lead, guide, direct, and empathize. Remember, a mentor has "been there and done that." A mentor can also guide a new principal without creating guilt, being judgmental, or imposing shame!

## Delving into the Research Literature

A key to further professional growth and development, a new principal, or, for that matter, any principal of tenure, must read the research literature. Why? (1) Data analysis acquired from research readings enhances instruction, improves learning, and develops appropriate and effective teaching and leading methods and techniques. (2) Research findings and/or conclusions based on empirical studies conducted with precision and integrity serve as critical links to more effective teaching and student-centered instructional practices.

Returning to the reading of research literature: According to Hudson-Barr (2004) and Subramanyam (2013), reading and delving into the research literature (1) ensures skill familiarity and mastery; (2) improves scientific literacy (the more read, the more learned; the more learned, the more critical assessing and understanding of empirical, scientific facts is likely to occur); (3) enhances newly applied learning; (4) improves career prospects; and (5) recognizes teaching, leading, and learning are ever changing. In other words, what was studied and learned yesterday may very well be further enhanced (changed for the better) by empirical, scientific research. Recall the adage: "Better to live and learn today than to die not knowing what could save a life" (in the case of the new principal, a professional life—your own!).

### *Examining the Research Literature Requires a Systematic and Logical Approach*

A simple yet informative guide, as noted below in items 1–3, can serve as a logical approach to reading the research literature, which in turn reaps significant rewards. For example, a new principal determined to learn to improve student achievement (1) decides to seek an idea for instructional or organizational improvement and thus turns to the research literature, (2) seeks a specified diagnosis or prognosis to enhance teaching and learning, or (3) simply desires the latest pragmatic information relative to innovative instructional updates.

Now, returning to the above-enumerated items, the rewards or benefits of reading and delving into the research literature will reveal (1) an idea for improved leadership discovered in an original research article, which in turn discloses research that examines either randomized, controlled, experimental, cohort, or case studies; (2) a meta-analysis, that is., a systematic combining of pertinent quantitative study data originating from several grounded (empirical) research studies; and (3) a review or analysis of research via a textbook, executive summary, or informative journal article based on previously conducted research studies. For example, a state principal association newsletter, periodical, or website can provide a new principal with current and relevant student-centered best practices.

Finally, recall the words of eighteenth-century English historian Edward Gibbon: "Let us read with method, and propose to ourselves an end to which our studies may point. The use of reading is to aid us in thinking" (BrainyQuote.com, 2022b). No truer words could be attributed to a new principal wishing to read the research literature and then learn from the data and analysis revealed.

## Presenting at Conferences: A Method of Advancing Self and Promoting Faculty

One surefire method of advancing self, and another key to professional growth and development, is for the new principal to respond to opportunities for making presentations at district professional development sessions as well as state and national conferences. To do so, the new principal is required to delve into the research literature; examine best practices from an instructional perspective; and recognize how student-centered teaching, leading, and learning are all adaptable to in-person or distance-learning presentations.

Serving as a presenter requires a gaining of essential knowledge and relevant expertise, boosts self-image and confidence, and also enhances self-persona, adding an aura of respect toward the principal, school, and district. Plus, others learn from a presenter and presentation, especially if members of the audience consider the presenter to be one of their own.

Additionally, new principals should seek opportunities to showcase the instructional team. Want to make a positive, morale-boosting impression on faculty and for faculty? Encourage teachers to join in on a presentation whereby they highlight specific teaching, best-practice, and student-centered instructional strategies, methods, and techniques. Engaged in an off-campus presentation, the team will have an opportunity to readily shine, look really fine, probably dine, and definitely feel divine!

## Writing for Publication: Express Expertise and Inform Others

Numerous vehicles for writing and publication are available for both principals and teachers. New principals, as a means of further professional growth and development, should seriously consider—during the course of the school year or during winter, spring, or summer breaks—writing about school leadership. The reasons for professional writing are numerous. Writing for publication (1) is critical to becoming a better instructional leader; (2) is the primary basis for sharing work experiences, knowledge gained, and learning achieved; (3) better equips a new principal with critical thinking skills; (4) expresses expertise; (5) fosters an ability to explain and refine ideas; (6) promotes self, school, and district; and (7) actually informs and entertains others!

## OVERCOMING ISOLATION

First, consider the date July 20, 1969, and the Apollo 11 flight when Neil Armstrong and Buzz Aldrin stepped out of the lunar landing module to walk on the surface of the moon. These two men were the first humans to do so. However, most people forget about a third important individual, Michael Collins, the astronaut who continued to fly the command module.

As Armstrong and Aldrin walked on the moon, Collins was isolated, alone within the spacecraft, orbiting. He was totally without communicative transmission abilities and thus unable to maintain contact with either of his two colleagues or NASA mission control. Not long into Collins's isolated flight, Mission Control in Houston, Texas, commented: "Not since Adam has any human known such solitude as Mike Collins" (Hayne, 2021).

Now think about the adage "It is lonely at the top!" Such a truism is quite apropos when considering the new principalship. First, the beginning principal is generally new to a campus. Second, relationship building is in its infancy stage. Third, the assistant principal is typically not a long-term acquaintance or friend. Fourth, faculty and staff have their own built-in/on-campus relationships and friendships. Typically, it takes a new principal three to four years to develop bonding relationships with faculty and staff.

Like that of astronaut Michael Collins when orbiting the moon, isolation for the new principal soon develops. Anxiety increases. Stress overwhelms. Loneliness is ever-present. Believe it or not, research reveals that the solitude of isolation actually impairs administrative function (Novotney, 2019). So, how does a new principal overcome isolation? Do the following as soon as possible for peace of mind as well as proper guidance and direction:

1. *Secure a mentor*. Already noted and stressed once again: If a mentor is not provided by the school district, find one.
2. *Network with other principals*. These people know the ropes. They may not appear to be interested in the welfare of a colleague—especially one that is beginning as a new principal—but most are generally kind, caring, and remember how that new principal experience was for them. Often, a networking principal colleague is one in an adjoining attendance zone or from a feeder campus, or one who is involved with a new principal on a district committee or in a community club, church, or synagogue. If that colleague, a soon-to-be-friend, does not reach out to you, reach out to them. A lifeline is nearby. Grab it!
3. *Incorporate good humor* to win over colleagues and gain friends. Everyone loves a good laugh as long as it is not at the expense of others. Joke and cajole. Faculty, staff, students, and even parents will appreciate a principal's humorous yet humble, reticent, and/or self-deprecating manner. Remember, laughter is the best medicine—especially when trying to make friends and get over loneliness!
4. *Reach out to a supervisor*. The best supervisors will have already reached out to the new principal. In case such has yet to occur, initiate the first step. Much can be gained and learned from the boss.
5. *Experience good interactions* with other school district leaders. Send a handwritten note or email expressing to the individual or individuals how much you appreciate their comradery, support, interaction, and expertise. Chances are, such a communiqué will initiate another opportunity to interact and possibly receive an invite to enjoy a free meal or, even better, develop a close, personal friendship!

*Note:* Sorenson and Goldsmith, frequently sourced within this text, served in the same school district as teachers, assistant principals, and principals. Early in their administrative careers, the two became close colleagues. Later, both served as university professors as well as co-authors of several books. To this day, some forty-five years later, they remain very close and the best of friends. This relationship exemplifies what can occur from experiencing good principal-colleague interactions.

## FINAL THOUGHTS

New principals must develop a plan of action to initiate Step #1: Advance Critical New Principal Skills for leader success. The plan of action should identify personal leadership strengths, establish a timeline for strengths to be enhanced, target leadership areas in need of development, and pinpoint specific techniques, methods, strategies, actions, and/or activities that will enhance principal leadership and capacity-building processes.

New principals must commit to a clear and doable vision, prioritize leadership skills, collaborate and coordinate with faculty, establish high expectations, and entrust tasks and responsibilities to faculty (always inspecting what is expected). New principals must be honorable, ethical, moral, credible, and legal, always pursuing guidance and advice and getting to know and understand learning community members.

New principals must always analyze data before making instructional decisions, be creative and take risks (always using good judgment), incorporate sound and effective communication skills, manage time and organizational abilities, and incorporate personal and career reflective, evaluative, and assessment practices.

New principals must acquire, possess, and utilize a strong set of critical skills for leadership success. Such skill sets include but are not limited to being change-oriented, demonstrating self-awareness, exhibiting discernment, understanding educational law and school board policies, managing school personnel, developing professional relationships, and interacting with students, parents, community members, and district professional staff and supervisors.

New principals must practice self-discipline, lead and follow, be inspirational and motivational, resolve conflict, learn by listening, be the lead learner, network, and always ask for help. To do so is surviving the leadership role. Burnout is real, often devastating, and more common than typically assumed.

New principals must recognize and initiate keys to personal and professional growth and development by taking care of self (mental, social, spiritual, emotional, and physical growth), and by finding a mentor—that individual who has "been there and done that." To better advance self and promote faculty, new principals should always consider presenting at conferences and writing for publication. Both express expertise and serve to inform others.

Finally, to overcome isolation, new principals must network with other principals, incorporate good humor to win over friends and colleagues, reach out to supervisors, and experience good and effective interactions with school district leaders.

## DISCUSSION QUESTIONS

1. Examine, early in the chapter, the three key aspects that must be considered or addressed as associated with a new principal's plan of action. Why are the three keys essential to plan development and new principal success?
2. Five new principal plan-of-action considerations and examples are identified. Which of the five do you perceive to be the most critical to a new principal's success? Justify your reasoning.
3. Examine the "Critical Leader Skills Identified: What's a New Principal to Do?" section and identify which ten of the thirty-plus skills listed would best initially aid a new principal. Explain why.
4. Noted within the chapter are fifteen "how and by what means" methods that can aid a new principal in overcoming the potential for failure and thus warrant early success. Review and then identify which seven of those listed could most enhance the success rate of a new principal. Support your responses.
5. Consider which of the seven identified Keys to Personal Growth and Development might best aid a new principal. Explain why.
6. Five steps to overcoming isolation are identified in the chapter. Which one of the five steps do you believe to be the most essential to surmounting isolation, anxiety, and overwhelming stress? Expound upon your response.

## CASE STUDY APPLICATION: WE NEED TO SET A FEW THINGS STRAIGHT!

Arturo Espinoza was new to Dr. Hugo Z. Hackenbush School. He was also a new principal as well as a second-generation immigrant, coming to the United States at the age of five. He had been chided by his father—a strong, vibrant man with little education but an amazing work ethic—to be the boss of the school. "Yes, Arturo, you are the boss now" his father prompted after learning his firstborn son had become a school principal. Arturo responded, "Papa, I will be the school leader—not a boss."

"No, *mijo*, you are the boss!" Arturo's father reiterated. Señor Espinoza then laughingly said, "My son, you know what a boss is, don't you?" "What, Papa?" Arturo asked. His father said, "You'll be a Double S—O—B, which is BOSS spelled backward!" The whole family laughed, as did Arturo! Arturo then sheepishly said, "Papa, I certainly hope not. Being a Double S—O—B is not a skill a new principal should ever possess or wish to use!"

Señor Espinoza always espoused a family creed: "¡*Familia, santa fe, y ser listo!*" ("Family, holy faith, and a good head!"). Each would come to pass, in career and life, during Arturo's first year as school principal. Arturo had recognized that it was important to not only lead but also to never forget family or his religious faith and to be level-headed in all actions and decisions.

"Welcome to Hackenbush School, Mr. Espinoza," said Flo Cortinas, campus secretary. Principal Espinoza walked into the administrative offices and greeted the campus secretary. Arturo was pleased and most honored to have been named the school's new principal. The easiest part of the job had been accomplished a couple of weeks earlier when Arturo had formally accepted the new principal position. Now he was on campus and administrative tasks were ready to be accomplished.

The first challenge of the first day was seated in the reception area, waiting grimly and expectedly. The campus secretary introduced one of the school's team leaders, Ms. Gloria Teasdale, who was unofficially and callously called by her peers and former school administrators—behind her back, of course—"*La Jefa*." Principal Espinoza had already been warned by his supervisors of the potential for the impending meeting. "Get ready," laughingly badgered one of the associate superintendents, saying, "*La Jefa*—the chief, the boss—she's coming your way. She'll be up in the saddle and atop her high horse!"

New principal Arturo Espinoza had practiced how he would deal with *La Jefa*, but now here she was, and she looked all but ready to pounce upon her new prey. Principal Espinoza swallowed his heart, which had somehow managed to rise up into his throat, and said, wide-eyed, "Good morning, Ms. Teasdale. Welcome. How can I be of assistance?" Gloria Teasdale stood up, grabbed his outreached hand, glared into the eyes of the new principal, and declared, "We need to set a few things straight before the school year begins!"

## Application Questions

1. Welcome to school, new principal—Mr. Arturo Espinoza—and what a welcome awaits you! Was "*La Jefa*'s" welcoming of the new principal to be expected? Possibly, since Mr. Espinoza was previously warned. However, consider Step #1: Advance Critical New Principal Skills and determine what specific skills or attributes could best be incorporated by the new principal when responding to Ms. Gloria Teasdale on that very first morning. Identify the skills selected and explain why those skills would be beneficial for the new principal.
2. Of the plan-of-action items listed in the chapter designed to guide a new principal, which of the examples noted might be most applicable to the new principal's first challenge? Clarify why.

3. Consider the "Critical Leader Skills Identified: What's a New Principal to Do?" listings and select five that new principal Arturo Espinoza needs to pull immediately out of his skills toolbox. Justify why the five were selected.
4. What aspect of the "Keys to Personal Growth and Development" section is most applicable to the first-day challenge—the first-hour situation obviously confronting Principal Espinoza? Relate why selected.
5. Reflect on the seven key points identified in the "Keys to Personal Growth and Development" section. In the scenario presented, which two "keys" could be of aid to the new principal?
6. Examine the chapter's concluding section, "Overcoming Isolation." Would any of the five concepts for conquering isolation actually relate to the case study scenario? If so, correlate how and by what means.

*Chapter 3*

# Step #2: The Leadership Absolutes Vital to Confidently Experiencing Today's Principalship

*Part 1: How to Identify, Acknowledge, and Incorporate the Seven Absolutes Essential to New Principal Success*

There need to be some absolutes in life!
(James E. Faust, American religious leader, lawyer, and politician, 1982)

When someone states there is no need for absolutes in leadership, then recognize this truism: Without absolutes, things can and will get worse!
(LuRella DeWray, education consultant, 2019)

### RECOGNIZE AND KNOW THE ABSOLUTES

Absolutes are defined as uncompromising, sometimes nonnegotiable fundamentals or principles which aid, if not guide and direct, a new principal. Absolutes, incorporating a guide and direction metaphor, are akin to a vehicle's GPS—a navigational tool. New principals have much to navigate as school leaders. These new administrators need tools to aid them in finding a roadway to leadership success. Absolutes are the required tools.

Identifying absolutes and avoiding obstacles and detours along the road to leadership success is no easy task. A primer with all the answers is difficult to come by. A successful long-term principal suggested that the answers for all new principals, beyond a primer, is a little OJT—on-the-job training! Now, on-the-job training has its place, but for new principals a "how-to" manual is essential.

The purpose of this text is to serve as that "primer"—a manual or handbook to guide new principals successfully around every busy corner, effortlessly over each speed bump, and avoiding those ever-jarring potholes, all obstacles along the leadership journey. Certain administrative practices and defined absolutes must first be recognized; second, incorporated, and third, successfully applied!

## THE NEW PRINCIPALSHIP: SEVEN LEADERSHIP ABSOLUTES

James F. Faust was correct in the opening quote: "There need to be some absolutes in life." New principals must recognize and understand the complexities of leading a school and come to a realization that certain "must-be-done" absolutes are ingrained aspects of the leadership role. Closely examined are seven leadership absolutes. New principals who follow Step #2, Part 1: How to Identify, Acknowledge, and Incorporate the Seven Absolutes Essential to New Principal Success can readily expect to achieve and flourish in the principalship.

### Absolute #1: The New Principal Serving as Lead Learner

Previously addressed in chapter 2, a new principal must be recognized as the lead learner. What is a lead learner? McKibben (2015) describes a lead-learner principal as one who is connected, creating networks, developing relationships, positively influencing, and always collaborating and learning with the community of learners. For example, if faculty or a faculty member is weak in literacy, the principal as lead learner must connect with said school personnel by seeking and sharing related research, initiating instructional best practices, modeling lessons, readily and constantly building up the individual or team, and collaboratively engaging all.

The lead learner is a facilitator, regularly leading teacher learning and development by directing their energies toward capacity building and helping pursue instructional improvement. To do so requires the new principal, as lead learner, to intensify focus on curriculum and instruction and to demonstrate to faculty what it means to be an effective, master teacher. Now, the question every new principal needs answered: "How is it accomplished?"

A how-to road map for success begins with the new principal (1) looking for and learning best teaching practices; (2) ensuring best practices are modeled; (3) establishing "co-leader" relationships with faculty; (4) shaping a culture that emphasizes learning and how to "work to learn" alongside teachers; (5) revealing how seizing upon instructional risks is part of the continuous learning process; (6) creating learning opportunities by interacting with students in classrooms, hallways, and/or the lunchroom, always discussing what students are reading and learning; and (7) organizing open conversations with parents about key curricular initiatives and instructional programs that best ensure parents are in the teaching and learning loop.

## Absolute #2: The New Principal Directing as Instructional Leader

Instructional leadership is all about understanding student differences, learning and motivation, effective teaching practices, classroom management, and assessing student learning. Today's classrooms are culturally diverse, many with language differences. It is essential that new principals have strong expertise and experiences in these areas.

New principals, as instructional leaders, must recognize that today's students come with differing cognitive and learning styles, are often multimodal (learning via multimedia research projects, educational games, or think-pair-share strategies, as well as case-based learning) and multi-literate (often literate in a home language and thus using linguistic and cultural experiences and diversity as sources of learning acquisition), and come from differing background experiences and thus must be instructed by and with culturally relevant pedagogy.

One additional consideration: New principals and teachers must recognize the numerous methods by which technology interacts and intertwines with a student's academic and personal life and therefore plan to actively gain control over the digital aspects of learning so common among students today. New principals and teachers must understand how technology and the digital world impact not only students but also teaching, social interaction, and professional development.

### *Special Education and the Inclusive School*

The new principal must play a pivotal role in leading all aspects of schooling, particularly relative to those students with disabilities who are served under the "Special Education" umbrella. More specifically, the new principal must be prepared to lead a school where inclusive education enables students with disabilities to have full access and participation, on an equal basis, in learning experiences and environments. The new principal must focus on inclusive school leadership by creating a climate of belonging where stakeholders value all students. Valuing all students includes a commitment to building a sense of belonging, welcoming diversity and differing backgrounds and experiences as well as learning abilities (McIntyre, 2022; Rose, n.d.). What is a new principal to do?

Identified are seven actions for a new principal to take relative to creating and developing an inclusive school: (1) Review the research literature to understand the best practice of inclusion. (2) Explicitly support the inclusive philosophy and practice. (3) Ensure that special education faculty are integrated within grade-level or departmental teams. (4) Provide planning time for general education and special education teachers to interact. (5) Ensure that all students, including those with disabilities, are participating in the school and district curriculum. (6) Convene meetings with both the general education and special education teachers being present. (7) Evaluate and present data indicating the amount of time special education students are spending in the general education classrooms and include data relevant to attendance, engagement, and achievement (McIntyre, 2022; Rose, n.d.).

*Program Supervision and Evaluation*

A collaborative approach to instructional leadership involves program supervision and evaluation. The new principal must understand there is a critical need for supervision and evaluation in schools today. It is a role and responsibility designed to help teachers, aid students, respond to parents, and guide/supervise school change and innovation. Program supervision and evaluation is all about the instructional leader conducting professional development, as well as collaboratively planning, monitoring, and evaluating the curriculum (Glickman, Gordon & Gordon, 2018).

Program supervision entails the new principal helping teachers plan for instruction, execute effective lessons, examine and evaluate lessons, manage classroom behaviors and expectations, conduct formal and informal observations, appropriately and effectively incorporate the research literature, and adapt to and frequently adopt new educational theories and instructional models (Aguilar & Cohen, 2022; Marzano et al., 2021).

One final message for the new instructional leader: It is critical to understand those curricular and instructional areas that will serve as student, teacher, and organizational strengths and, at the same time, determine how to cope with those areas of weakness that will create stress for the learning community, including the principal. Program supervision and evaluation, as detailed, is the one aspect of instructional leadership by which a new principal and team can beat the ever-pervading stress factor and the exclusionary practices being preached today by outside forces.

*It's a Wild New World Out There, and Adaptation Is Essential*

New principals must adapt to changing social mores and thus have at least a basic knowledge and understanding of gender differences, gender bias, transgenderism, gender-nonconforming, gender identity, sexual orientations, and LGBTQ+ issues—all deemed controversial by many parents, policymakers, and legislators. All identified serve as adaptation challenges for instructional leaders, new principals or not.

Moreover, new principals may very well be confronted by serious political ideologies, partisan divides, race and racism, extremist agendas, parental rights, concerned citizen groups, censorship efforts, book bans, teacher voice restrictions, constrictive contributions of women and people of color, as well as the interjection of inequities and inequalities, along with Second Amendment rights advocates, gun control, pro-life/pro-choice positions, immigrant rights, critical race theory, parent rights in curriculum and/or school choice—a list that goes on and on (see chapter 4, "Incivility, the Lack of Public Decorum, and Survival Tactics," and i"Controversial Issues"). Just a reminder: The principalship is not easy!

Just a few years back, when examining instructional leadership for the twenty-first century, a brief review of identified critical issues makes no mention of any of the previously identified instructional leadership concerns, considerations, and controversies. Yes, it is a wild new world out there for the first-year principal. Ready to adapt? Ready to accept the challenges? Ready to lead? Ready to boldly step onto what some call a fine line when it comes to the service of all students equally and equitably? Ready or not (and the new principal had better be ready to lead, with all students-first convictions), here come the trials, tests, and demanding tasks of leading!

## Absolute #3: The New Principal Surrounding Self with a "Forward-Thinking," "Can-Do," and "Ready-to-Get-It-Done" Leadership Team

The new principal must work to surround self with a leadership team—assistant principal(s), instructional coaches, secretary, and even office personnel—who command personalities that are focused, driven, organized, competitive, achievement-oriented, efficient, successful, detail-oriented, adaptable, flexible, deadline-sensitive, time managers, goal-oriented, take-charge, relationship-oriented, friendly, moral, ethical, and loyal and who possess high expectations of self and others.

Identifying and finding all the identified traits in one person is probably impossible. However, employing differing individuals in different leadership team positions with some of the noted characteristics will only enhance the success of a learning community as well as that of the new principal. Recognize also that such individuals and personalities will not necessarily be inherited upon arrival in the new leadership position. Achieving leadership personnel with at least some of the noted personality traits and skills will take time, patience, in-depth interviewing, and development of hiring practices that ensure an appropriate selection process.

Finally, a new principal must never hesitate to employ individuals on the leadership team who are more intelligent than he or she is. These team members should frequently be different thinkers, perceive different solutions to problems or issues, and be effective decision-makers (Driscoll, 2023).

## Absolute #4: The New Principal Supervising School Personnel

A school's principal and personnel are the number-one determiner of student and organizational success. For the new principal, quality personnel leadership is crucial to effective person-to-person on-campus interactions as well as developing trust, respect, honesty, responsibility, rights, and expectations. The school's principal, as personnel manager, must possess strong communication skills and develop open communicative avenues and opportunities for teacher-to-student, teacher-to-teacher, teacher-to-all stakeholders, teacher-to-parent, and principal-to-teacher communications.

Effective personnel management and human resources administration encompasses conflict resolution, recruitment and selection, and induction and mentoring programs in addition to addressing and working through adverse situations—a short list with potential for lengthy repercussions. One final introductory remark: Working with school personnel can be a difficult prospect for new principals who neither anticipate nor prepare for the numerous challenges, persistent individual needs, and unremitting circumstances that evolve when confronted with the responsibility of maintaining and improving the capabilities of a campus workforce.

### *Leading Personnel Is Hard Work*

Teachers can create both challenges and opportunities for any new principal. Ready for the difficult task of leading, guiding, and directing school personnel? One new principal laughingly joked, "It's like herding cats!" Well, it can certainly be trial by fire at times, but there is good reason to recognize that school personnel are a new principal's best prospect of successfully navigating the murky waters of schooling. Personnel, often a bane to any principal, can also be a much-needed lifeline in the turbulent seas of troubled leadership.

## Stress Makes for Hard Work and, by the Way, Who Needs It?

*Education Week* reports that studies continue to mount relative to teachers and the stress factor. A RAND Corporation study revealed that nearly 60 percent of teachers report they are stressed, burned out, in comparison to 44 percent for other workers (Sparks, 2022). To further complicate teaching, leading, and learning, the teaching profession status is at a fifty-year low (Peetz, 2022).

The good news: Gewertz (2021) recommends five methods by which principals can aid teachers with mental health issues: (1) Talk regularly about mental health. (2) Train the administrative team in how to note early signs of mental health struggles in teachers. (3) Create ongoing systems of support, that is, circles of support as well as virtual groups. (4) Build a culture of genuine inquiry regarding team members. (5) Recognize that certain employee groups can very well need more support than others, that is, Black, Latinx, and LGBTQ+ employees. Never assume that all employees need the same supports or services.

Advice for the new principal when it comes to personnel and mental health considerations: Life is precarious. Never presume all is well. Every individual has serious issues to overcome—some more weighty, if not more dire, than others. Yes, leading personnel is hard work!

## Interacting with the Best

Many years ago, Sears, Roebuck and Company offered a variety of house paints simply described as "good," "better," and "best." The company's "best" paint makes for an exceptional analogy: Like that best paint, the best teachers are high-quality, easy to work with, versatile, high-performing, long-lasting, and durable. They also fix mistakes; offer something for everyone; maintain their luster; are fade-resistant, nonferrous (don't possess a hardened personality), and easy to manage; and stand the test of time. The best paint descriptors illustrate what a new principal can expect when interacting with the best teachers!

## Interacting with Those in Need of Assistance

Many teachers, as previously described, fall into the categories of good, better, and best. Regrettably, however, there are teachers who may not have a good command of instruction. These teachers are not to be discarded, moved from grade level to grade level, placed in a less instructionally oriented setting, or simply transferred. Teachers in need of assistance require a principal's personal and professional attention, including but not limited to being positive, uplifting, and encouraging, while never negating expectations.

Ensuring that an employee's self-esteem remains intact is easier said than done, especially for a new principal. Guidelines for helping personnel in need of assistance include (1) acting quickly and responsibly; (2) making crystal clear that expectations are not being met; (3) advising, in sufficient detail, how instruction is inadequate, deficient, or unsatisfactory; (4) providing a reasonable response time for performance improvement; (5) modeling effective teaching strategies, techniques, methods, and practices; (6) offering teacher-to-teacher observations (permit a teacher in need of assistance to observe a very best, master teacher); and (7) stipulating—following classroom observations and related documentation, as an appraisal system dictates—the availability of an appeal process.

## Supervising Marginal Teachers

New principals must be prepared to closely observe and aid marginal employees and, moreover, understand what is deemed unsatisfactory performance criteria. Sorenson and Goldsmith (2009) describe marginal teachers as those who (1) fail to teach the mandated curriculum; (2) fail to exhibit an interest in or dedication toward students and/or teaching; (3) fail to exhibit interpersonal skills with students and colleagues; (4) fail to demonstrate effective and appropriate instructional skills; (5) fail to maintain an organized classroom, lessons, and plans; (6) fail to establish expectations for student management and behavior; or (7) fail to exhibit knowledge of the subject matter. Teacher instructional failure in any of the seven identified areas equates to marginal teaching practices and, thus, teachers who are in need of assistance.

## Engaging with Teacher Resisters

Resisters are found in every profession. They obviously have their reasons for protesting or dissenting, especially when it comes to a proposed reform. In education, resistance frequently occurs when change is in the air. Personnel simply do not like change. Well, that is not completely true. The only change people truly like is the change that jingles in their pocket! There will always be individual resisters who are typically known at school as the campus malcontents, nonconformist, or complainers. New principals must be aware that there are also individual resisters who have a reason to voice a concern about a proposed change or reform. So, as is often the case, the critical question is: "What's a new principal to do?"

A series of tactics work when responding to resisters: (1) Know what teachers want and need (power and recognition). (2) Know what teachers do (they resist, sabotage, deny, and delay). (3) Know why teachers become cynical and resist instructional change (they want proper planning and preparation before a change is made). (4) Know how to respond to resisters (recognize there are essential strategies when engaging resisters). (5) Know how to build shared knowledge (initiate professional development). (6) Know how to effect positive change and overcome teacher resistance by incorporating principal resiliency (lead, lead, lead). (7) Know that principals must also change if resistance is a regular feature on campus.

Finally, a brief but exceptional read for the new principal is *Responding to Resisters: Tactics That Work for Principals* (Sorenson, 2021). This book provides the new principal with essential information and associated tools necessary when engaging campus resisters and initiating required change.

*Managing Personnel and Adverse Circumstances*

As previously noted, leading school personnel is hard work. So, what's a new principal to do? Research has long proven that attempting to motivate personnel or improve morale through fear or intimidation does not work, especially with marginal teachers (Hewertson, 2020; Hughes, Ginnett, & Curphy, 2021; Norton, 2015, 2017; Sorenson & Goldsmith, 2009).

What does work is following a series of guidelines: (1) Regularly consult and follow the personnel section of school board policy as well as administrative procedures and regulations when working with personnel in need of assistance. (2) Be proactive, and take corrective actions as required. (3) Establish and maintain performance expectations. (4) Document, document, document! Remember, an adverse personnel incident never occurred unless it was documented.

Continuing a listing of principal personnel guidelines: (5) Know the law and always apply due process. (6) Recognize controversial personnel issues such as discrimination, sexual harassment, alcohol and drug use and abuse, incompetence, immorality, violent and unprofessional conduct, insubordination, misappropriation of public funds, criminal violations, and obtaining district services for personal benefit. (7) Understand union-management relationships, contracts for public school employees, organizational security, compensation and working conditions, the grievance process, and individual security (Sorenson & Goldsmith, 2009).

A final statement regarding the new principal as a manager of school personnel: An exceptional handheld, brief, single-topic-focused book that every new principal should have in their office is *The Principal's Guide to Managing School Personnel* (Sorenson & Goldsmith, 2009). This is not only a classic read and bestseller but also a most enlightening source of helpful information when working with teachers and staff.

## Absolute #5: The New Principal Managing School Operations

Sharp and Walter (2012) strongly stipulate that the new principal must manage the school budget, ensure building maintenance is a priority, develop positive community relations, understand and follow educational law as well as district policies and regulations, maintain proper and effective student discipline, establish strong school safety standards, and develop the master schedule.

New principals must confirm procedures for daily transportation and bus safety, recognize the importance of the school breakfast and lunch programs, develop the assistant principal role, ensure that all special education regulations are followed, schedule and conduct regular and effective walk-throughs, and safeguard a healthy school environment (both school wellness and well-being programs).

Sharp and Walter (2012) also contend that a new principal will never survive for any length of time as an instructional leader if the mundane tasks of maintaining a clean, safe, and properly managed school are overlooked or neglected. Bottom line: New principals must not only serve as an instructional leader but also be an effective school operations manager.

## Absolute #6: The New Principal Ensuring a Safe and Secure Learning Community

Next to last in the "Absolutes" listing, but by no means least, is school safety and security. New principals must be aware of the ever-pervasive threat to the lives of students, faculty and staff, and learning community members. Much has been reported and detailed via news media, social networking, and informative writings. However, school safety remains more than a concern today. It is absolutely critical that school safety and security be in the forefront of every new principal's mind. Danger lurks!

There have been 169 school shootings since 2018. During the 2021–22 school year, fifty-one school shootings happened in the United States, the most in any single year. In January 2023 a staggering seven school shootings occurred. At this rate, there could very well be more than eighty school shootings across the nation prior to the end of the 2023 school year. Last year (2022) there was a total of 647 mass shootings in America (*Education Week*, 2023).

Another set of alarming statistics from the *Wall Street Journal* reveal that in January 2023 alone, 2.6 million firearm background checks (a proxy for measuring gun sales) occurred in the United States. The top three states conducting arms sales background checks were Texas (121,594), Pennsylvania

(100,769), and Illinois (88,501). The bottom five (least to most) were Hawaii (1,847), Rhode Island (2,059), Vermont (3,244), Delaware (4,006), and Wyoming (4,109). The vast majority of these arms background checks were for handguns (Stebbins, 2023).

Our country is plagued with a handgun and automatic rifle disease, and school students and teachers are often the victims. Regardless of politics, it is impossible to overlook or brush aside the tragedies of life taken in school shootings. The "why" question is one that could be debated for days on end and with what seems to be, at least today, no resolution. A lifesaving fact: Every possible action and precaution must be taken by every new principal to ensure the safety and security of learning communities.

Two excellent resources for new principals relative to this topic are the National Association of School Psychologists' "Responding to School Violence: Tips for Administrators" (2021) and the National Association of Secondary School Principals' (NASSP) "NASSP School Safety Resources" (2022). In addition, a Google search will provide new principals with relevant and up-to-date information regarding violence in schools as well as school safety and security procedures.

## Absolute #7: The New Principal Enduring Emergent Forces

Enduring emerging forces serves as an absolute for the new principal. Such forces include but are not limited to pandemic aftereffects, teacher shortages, activist parents, incivility and lack of public decorum, technology, social media effects, and controversial issues. In chapter 4, each of these identified and emerging forces are closely examined relative to the new principal's role and responsibility.

*A Point to Ponder*

Consider this adage: "If one chooses to ignore all the absolutes, such comes at a price!" Reading the first three chapters of this book has already laid the essential groundwork for new principal success. An initial survey of the road ahead has been conducted. That is the good news! The great news? While the road to success is often long, sometimes rough and bumpy, and frequently arduous with numerous potential detours, new principals must persevere, be tenacious, and follow one of the rules of the road—Step #2, Part 1: How to Identify, Acknowledge, and Incorporate the Seven Absolutes Essential to New Principal Success.

In the forthcoming chapters, be ready to experience even more insightful leadership passageways. Be prepared, journeyman/woman, to travel and encounter, with ample directions, new and different principal-oriented highways and byways!

## FINAL THOUGHTS

New principals must integrate Step #2, Part 1: How to Identify, Acknowledge, and Incorporate the Seven Absolutes Essential to New Principal Success into their leadership toolbox. Absolute #1: The new principal serves as the lead learner. Absolute #2: The new principal directs as the instructional leader. Absolute #3: The new principal surrounds self with a strong and effective leadership team. Absolute #4: The new principal supervises school personnel. Absolute #5: The new principal manages school operations. Absolute #6: The new principal ensures a safe and secure learning community. Absolute #7: The new principal more than endures. The new principal actually overcomes each of the seven emergent forces facing education today.

Now, read and reflect on chapter 4 and how the noted seven emerging forces apply to the new principal role. Aways consider the ever-present question: "What's a principal to do?"

## DISCUSSION QUESTIONS

1. New principals must recognize the obstacles and know the absolutes as identified in Step #2, Part 1: How to Identify, Acknowledge, and Incorporate the Seven Absolutes Essential to New Principal Success. Of the seven leadership absolutes, which one do you perceive to be most critical to the overall success of a new principal? Explain why.
2. Review each of the seven leadership absolutes essential to new principal success. Identify what a new principal must do, first, to become (a) a lead learner, (b) an instructional leader, (c) a leader of a competent leadership team, (d) a supervisor of school personnel, (e) a manager of school operations, (f) a protector of a safe and secure learning community, and (g) a leader enduring emergent forces (for more about this absolute, see chapter 4).
3. Examine Absolute #4: The New Principal Supervising School Personnel. Carefully review each of the section's subheadings: (a) Leading personnel is hard work. (b) Stress makes for hard work and, by the way, who needs it? (c) Interacting with the best. (d) Interacting with those in need of assistance. (e) Supervising marginal teachers. (f) Engaging with teacher resisters. (g) Managing personnel and adverse circumstances.

Identify what is essential, if not crucial, in each of the subheadings relative to a new principal's success.
4. Reflect upon the final chapter section, "A Point to Ponder," and the quote "If one chooses to ignore all the absolutes, such comes at a price!" Now, place yourself in the role of a new principal. Doing so, select one of the seven absolutes essential to new principal success and contemplate the leadership repercussions of not following the identified absolute. Provide a detailed response.
5. What is the principal of your campus doing to best ensure Absolute #6: The New Principal Ensuring a Safe and Secure Learning Community, specifically as it relates to gun violence (school shootings)? Share your response with other class or book study members.

## CASE STUDY APPLICATION: IS THE CHALLENGE AN OPPORTUNITY, OR IS THE OPPORTUNITY A CHALLENGE?

Longtime principal T. G. Culpepper, now retired, sat in the administrative office at Tyler Fitzgerald School across the desk from the new principal, Madlyn Schwartz. Culpepper had long been called "The Chief." The Chief had been selected as a principal coach for Madlyn. As a new teacher some years ago, Madlyn had experienced leadership command from The Chief when she taught history at his school. Those days were long passed, and now new principal Schwartz looked to The Chief for guidance. She exclaimed, "Chief, I'm not certain whether this challenge is an opportunity or this opportunity is a challenge."

The Chief smiled and said, "I suspect, Madlyn, that it's a little of both, don't you think?" Principal Schwartz gave a worried smile and replied, "Yes, sir, it is." The Chief continued, "You do realize, Madlyn, leaders are made and not born. Sometimes leaders are made under pressure, so you are not alone. Others have been where you are today, and you, like them, will ultimately succeed."

Madlyn quickly reflected on her new role as an instructional leader. It had been, in Madlyn's words, "a doozy of a time!" Confronted with one challenge after another, the principal's self-care could best be described as an "empty glass." Taking time to invest in herself and away from the new principalship role had been minimal. A mistake, yes, she understood.

That was just one of many mistakes the new principal had made. It seemed that some of those mistakes had included indecision. The Chief had told her, "Madlyn, you must recognize that indecision itself is a decision, and not a good one. You must seek input from and collaborate with those teachers who are masters at the work they do and seek guidance and help from those you trust most. Be curious, Madlyn; ask questions, use good judgment and discernment, and never be afraid to lead." Madlyn nodded in the affirmative. It had been a long year, and the first semester was yet to be completed!

Madlyn then asked, "How do I turn the challenges I am facing into opportunities and not turn opportunities into challenges?" The Chief responded, "First, Madlyn, identify for me your challenges thus far and, of those challenges, which ones are eating your lunch!"

The new principal began to recount her challenges as the new school leader, focusing on the one that was giving her the most trouble. Turning to The Chief, Madlyn said, "This challenge just began recently. I've tried to work with the teacher, but I seem to be getting nowhere. This teacher has four issues: First, he is not coming to work on a regular basis, and it is becoming a consistent pattern—every Monday and Friday, making for a nice four-day weekend. The teacher claims to have some undetermined illness.

"Second," Principal Schwartz shared, "the teacher, when at work, does not properly supervise his students. He disappears for ten to twenty minutes at a time, leaving students unattended. He claims he must go to the restroom and attend to his health matter. However, it has been reported to me that he has actually been going to the workroom, not the restroom, and leisurely interacting with other teachers. I have notified our district personnel director, but she states that she is overwhelmed with matters from other schools that are much more demanding."

The principal continued: "Third, Chief, the teacher is anything but civil in his interactions with me. He is rude, disrespectful, loud, and downright lacking in civility. Sir, I'm at a loss!

"Fourth, and finally, the teacher is believed to be making less than appropriate statements to students, some of which I perceive to be racist."

T. G. Culpepper interjected: "Let's start with one challenge at a time. Number 1: The teacher is not reporting to work on a regular basis and seems to be enjoying four-day weekends at the expense of his students, not to mention the new principal. He's taking advantage, so let's make it a disadvantage for him. Let me give you a quick seven-point plan," her mentor replied. "Here goes," he said:

- "First, focus on the issue, the problem. How can the absenteeism be overcome?
- "Second, drill down. Determine a viable solution to the problem.
- "Third, make a list of exactly what needs to occur to resolve the issue. Identify who needs to be involved in reaching a solution. Recognize there is a problem within the problem—the personnel director, unfortunately, is not available. That, however, is a problem to be worked out

another day. I have a suggestion for a resolution to that particular problem, which I'll share with you later.
- "Fourth, always seek opportunities to brainstorm, ask questions, and seek answers. Begin by interacting with your administrative team and your campus secretary. You know the old saying, Madlyn: The two most important individuals on a campus are the school secretary and the custodian! Receive essential input from helpful parties. Also, you have been given a mentor. That's me! So take advantage of my expertise. What this particular obstacle has done so far is create a confusing complication, overwhelm you with a problem you don't need, and, once again, generate indecision.
- "Fifth, flip challenges into opportunities by forming a list of strategies and potential solutions and resolutions. Then prepare to execute a plan of action.
- "Sixth, execute the plan of action. Take the essential steps toward success and achievement. Recognize that every challenge can become an opportunity for success. Now, let's recognize that some challenges are small, and some are big. Work takes time, and solutions take work. Persevere. Move forward. Reflect daily. Learn from every scenario. Tenacity makes for success! Recall the words of Louis Pasteur: 'Let me tell you the secret that has led me to my goal. My strength lies solely in my tenacity' (AZQuotes.com, 2022a).
- "Seventh, last but not least, follow the prescribed Seven Absolutes Essential to Success that I shared with you earlier this semester. Put the absolutes to work for the benefit of students, teachers, and, yes, the new principal."

Principal Madlyn Schwartz stood up from behind her desk, gave The Chief a big grin, and then walked around to where The Chief was seated. Madlyn gave him a big pat on the back, saying, "Sir, you've made my day!"

The Chief replied, "We'll solve the problems you face," then grinned back at the new principal and said, "See, sometimes I'm good for something!"

## Application Questions

1. Examine "The Chief's" seven-point plan designed to turn challenges into opportunities. Which of the seven points would best aid Principal Madlyn Schwartz considering the new leadership challenges she faces? Detail why.
2. Which of the seven absolutes most readily applies to the principal and, specifically, to the teacher issue? Explain why and provide, from your chapter reading, a probable solution.

3. Consider the first six points of The Chief's seven-point plan. Determine which of the six points best correlate with each of the four problems facing Principal Schwartz. Defend your responses.
4. Finally, is the challenge before Principal Schwartz an opportunity, or is the opportunity a challenge? Explain your answer.

*Chapter 4*

# Step #2: The Leadership Absolutes Vital to Confidently Experiencing Today's Principalship

## *Part 2: Absolute #7: How to Successfully Endure, Transcend, and Survive the Seven Emergent Forces Challenging the New Principal Role*

> Where there is no struggle, there is no strength!
> (Oprah Winfrey, BrainyQuote.com, 2023)

### THE EMERGENT FORCES: WHAT ARE THEY? WHO ARE THEY? WHY ARE THEY?

Oprah Winfrey hit the nail on the head when she stated, "Where there is no struggle, there is no strength." The new principal will meet head-on the struggles of dealing with emergent forces in education. These forces often pressure the new principal to not only struggle but also persevere. However, with every struggle comes a renewed strength, even when that strength does not seem to appear at the time of a particular challenge. New principals, everywhere, must face the headwinds of emergent forces. It is part of the job. However, being prepared to endure and then enduring to survive is paramount, and such efforts will bring forth the essential strengths necessary to succeed.

Emergent forces: The "What are they" was identified in the concluding paragraph of chapter 3 and will be further explored in the next section, "Seven Emerging Forces." Now the question becomes "Who are they?" Emergent forces are those powers, energies, dynamisms, influences, or imposing drivers or initiatives that come into being—some are simple yet good; some are effectual, with positive and lasting consequences; and others are strong or robust but, as a result, disparaging or damaging.

For example, in the early 1990s new and different technologies began to materialize with an expectation of worldwide incorporation and significance, as well as ongoing use in the near future. The internet was at that time, and remains so today, an emergent force—making a serious and most imposing, long-lasting, and influential impact.

Why are emergent forces influential and instrumental in education? During and following the COVID-19 pandemic, the educational scenario changed unpredictably. Educators at all levels found that remaining unadaptable in the midst of the emerging COVID-related forces was unproductive at best. However, being adaptable yet reticent was not helpful either. Adaptability had to be more than being safe, secure (maintaining the status quo), and risk-adverse.

Adaptability then was all about being aggressive, unconfined, and persevering as an opportunist. Adaptability today is not only recognizing but understanding that emergent forces can be positive and effective. However, at times emergent forces must be attentively handled and managed and, furthermore, recognized as often being a negative for the new principal and learning community and thus a reason for caution.

New principals must acknowledge not only the benefits of emergent forces but the associated challenges as well. New principals must realize the "why." Simply, emergent forces serve as impetuses for further developing and enhancing effective learning environments in which principals, teachers, administrative team members, and instructional coaches convey and share knowledge in a most effective manner and, at the same time, promote potential changes and necessary reforms. Such is the reasoning for the "Why are they?" query.

## SEVEN EMERGING FORCES

Following are seven emerging forces in education today.

### Pandemic Aftereffects

The Brown Center, in collaboration with the Brookings Institute (Kuhfeld et al., 2022), reports that the pandemic, as an emerging force in education, has had and continues to have a devastating impact on learning. First, reading and math test scores dropped considerably. Second, test-score gaps between students in low-poverty and high-poverty schools increased by 20 percent in math and 15 percent in reading. Third, schools experienced high rates of absenteeism, with students missing increased days.

Also, and readily associated with the pandemic and aftereffects, the high levels of absenteeism posed a highly significant problem for students, parents, and school personnel. Low student attendance, driven at the time by quarantine policies, debilitated instructional reforms, and disrupted teaching and learning. Yet, struggles with absenteeism existed before the pandemic and remain a constant to this day! Principals, teachers, and parents must work together to create a stronger and more effective focus on student attendance.

Noted, absences frequently result from painful yet rational choices between a family's basic well-being and attending school. This creates a spiraling process that can evolve into a crisis for family and schools. While everyone recognizes that attendance is a priority, it never outweighs the need for family shelter, food, safety, and reliable child care. Regrettably, the problem does and will exist for new principals. Unfortunately, the list for possible solutions is long but remains short on results (Levin & Bakuli, 2022).

Fourth, students and educators continue to struggle with mental health challenges. Fifth, higher rates of violence and misbehaviors continue to occur in schools. Domestic violence during COVID reached unimaginable heights (Mineo, 2022). Additionally, the Centers for Disease Control and Prevention (CDC) reports that teen girls, during and following COVID, are caught in an overwhelming wave of sadness and violence (Edwards, 2023). Finally, an increase in lost instructional time remains a struggle for many school systems (Kuhfeld et al., 2022).

Pandemic aftereffects and the bottom line: According to Dorn, Hancock, Sarakatsannis, and Viruleg (2022), unfinished learning is real and inequitable, and the harm inflicted by the pandemic goes beyond academics and is related to clinical mental health conditions (lost family members, lost jobs and sources of income, social isolation, and continued inflationary costs, for example). Obviously, unfinished learning will continue to have a long-term impact with serious consequences (for example, lower earnings, lower levels of education attainment, and less innovation).

Again, the question: "What's a new principal to do?" (1) Reengage students and reenroll students into effective teaching and learning environments. (2) Support students in recovering unfinished learning and aid with mental health care and funding. (3) Recommit to and reimagine what education can be over the long haul. (4) Effectively and appropriately utilize government funding for schools and students.

New principals can also wage their "honeymoon" time by pressing school district leaders to readily use the 2021 American Rescue Plan funds as well as Elementary and Secondary School Emergency Relief (ESSER III) and other succeeding federal funding to expand staff, reduce class size, recruit new teachers and academic specialists at higher rates of pay, and retain current staff by offering retention bonuses specifically targeting acute needs.

Current and future federal funding can offer across-the-board pay increases, pay additional stipend funding for increased workloads (tutoring, for example), improve working conditions (enhancing culture and climate), assist with overcoming high absenteeism rates, and augment professional development for literacy-specific needs. (Interestingly, according to National Student Support Accelerator, 2021, as schools and school districts are utilizing federal funding for tutoring, student learning is not only increasing, but principals are finding new approaches to not only link tutoring to instruction and increased student achievement but also embed tutoring into the instructional day.)

Federal funds can also enrich social and emotional learning for mental health issues and ensure that radical attention is provided to special education students and English language learners and their needs and that increased attention is paid relative to equity, equality, diversity, and civic education and learning. Finally, federal dollars can aid in implementing advancements of technology and digital learning (Jordan & Dimarco, 2022).

Yet there is a caveat: Recognize that postpandemic funds will inevitably fade, potentially bringing about reduced federal funding and the conceivable cutting of programs, laying off of staff, asking of voters to approve higher tax rates or increased bond programs, or, at the very least, overhauling of district and school budgets in order to safeguard essential services (Lieberman, 2023).

## Teacher Shortages, Quiet Quitting, and the Great Resignation

Following two years of pandemic health measures, teachers across America are walking away from their schools by the hundreds of thousands, vowing never to return. The National Center for Education Statistics found that 44 percent of public schools reported teacher vacancies/shortages. The number of teachers quitting in June 2022 was almost 41 percent higher than the previous year (Querolo, Rockeman, & Ceron, 2022). One teacher, in particular, spent her final two years as a teacher quiet quitting. Today that teacher is an employee at Costco, reporting that there is life after teaching and that life is actually better now. She revealed that she is finally sleeping at night (Hart, 2023). A sad commentary relative to teaching as a profession today.

Additionally, a February 2022 Gallup Poll revealed that K–12 educators were the most burned-out segment of the US labor force. To fill the vacancies, school districts have resorted to permitting veterans and other noncredentialed employees to serve as teachers. Some districts have actually reduced the school week to four days (Berger, 2022).

Most alarming, more than half the nation's teachers are seeking opportunities to exit the profession. The reasons: low pay, lack of respect, bad behavior from both parents and students, overworked, teaching virtually, and continued health risks associated with teaching in person. Teachers are telling family members, neighbors, and undergraduate students in teacher education programs to strongly consider a different career (Miller, 2022).

To top all previously noted, teachers—along with a significant number of the workforce nationwide—are actively engaging in "quiet quitting." Quiet quitting is a process by which teachers are extending no more effort in their jobs than absolutely necessary. Quiet quitting, across the nation, is definitely a wake-up call for superintendents, principals, and district human resources departments.

Quiet quitting is a sweeping phenomenon associated with low pay; lack of respect at work; childcare issues; inflexible hours (teachers desiring part-time work and three-day weekends); less than adequate benefits, most notably associated with increases in healthcare premiums and prescription drugs; insufficient medical services; as well as work stress and pressures along with student and parent misbehaviors.

The question, once again: "What's a new principal to do?" First, recognize the teacher shortage problem cannot be resolved by any one person. The shortage is an institutional problem—one that has been left to fester for far too long at the expense of teachers and, most certainly, students. Second, understand that a new principal can positively impact the teacher shortage and quiet quitting not only by focusing on improved culture and climate and on recruitment processes and procedures but also by initiating retention efforts and programs.

Recent studies conducted by RAND Corporation reveal that teachers are more than stressed. They are depressed. Seventy-five percent of teachers nationwide are not coping well with job-related stress. They really do not wish to leave the profession, but they are finding it more and more difficult to find joy in their work (Will, 2022).

Furthermore, one-third of the teacher respondents report they are likely to leave their current teaching position at the end of the school year. District leaders and principals must take that intent to leave seriously, because even if the teachers contemplating leaving do not leave, the issues of job satisfaction and quiet quitting are significant signs of employee dissatisfaction and thus remain obstacles to retention and service.

Again, "What's a new principal to do?" First, recognize that teacher and staff well-being is a serious issue. Teachers need support with student academic learning and achievement; management of student misbehaviors; the expectancy of having to take way too much work home; the requirement to fulfill additional workloads, inducing additional before and after hours at school; the continuous handling of irate and disrespectful parents; and a continual year-in, year-out insufficient salary, even with pay increases. Plus, poor mental health is a major concern.

School districts must also seek better healthcare plans that are all about patients and services and not so much about district savings and health insurance company profits. Profits above patients has become a twenty-first-century dilemma for consumers. Major corporations, big pharma, insurance companies, even school districts seem to focus on dollars first and service—and customer and employee satisfaction—last! Until these problems are addressed and resolved, principals must recognize that teachers are burdened, anxious, and sick and tired of the status quo. Teachers need both mental and emotional assistance! So, once again, "What's a new principal to do?"

Considering there is often a disconnect between what teachers need and what districts are offering, the RAND Corporation submits the following recommendations: (1) Develop a positive school environment. (2) Ensure that teachers feel supported and involved in decision-making. (3) Foster positive relationships with teachers and staff. (4) Offer better and closer attention to teachers' needs and requests. (5) Provide confidential access to mental health supports (most districts should have related plans).

The RAND Corporation further recommends: (6) Provide wellness programs during school hours—not after school, when teachers either need to pick up children, could really use after hours for grading and lesson planning, or are simply worn out from lengthy instructional days and efforts. (7) Always understand that as the school leader, a gentle—other times, a firm—push of upper-level administration is required to better ensure appropriate well-being actions are taken (*The Master Teacher*, 2018).

Teaching is one of the most thankless jobs in America, often a career filled with limited value, regard, and admiration, as well as long hours and harried treatment. A new principal must show great respect for faculty and recognize teachers as heroes, pushing for hero days, heroes of the month, heroes of the year, and then rewarding those heroes—monetarily (and make it worthwhile). Public recognition in newspapers, television reports, convocations, and faculty meetings is essential. A kind note, a pat on the back, and/or a commending handshake can help make a positive difference as an initial start to overcoming teacher shortages and quiet quitting and therefore help prevent those great heroes from becoming part of the Great Resignation.

**Activist Parents**

Parental involvement in schools today is rapidly moving from traditional parent-teacher organizations or associations to a different kind of parental engagement—activism. Parental involvement today is often very different from the work of a school's PTO or PTA, which are in decline nationwide. Instead of raising funds for the school to purchase playground equipment or stage curtains, parents are much more likely to be rallying around some political theme or candidate (usually for the school board), drafting legislative language, aiding in book bans, or lobbying for a specific political agenda.

Activist parents no longer place posters or cards in storefront windows announcing the school's fall festival. Instead they are utilizing the internet, posting on social media, videoconferencing, and/or attending conferences backed by donors of like mind. So, who are these activist parents and how might a new principal be impacted? Many are political ideologists attempting to either gain or maintain political power. Following are examples of parental activist groups that are frequently observed across the nation:

- Conservative/right-wing parents pushing back against perceived cultural shifts (e.g., Moms for Liberty, Manhattan Institute–Woke Schooling for Concerned Parents, Citizens Renewing America, 1776 Project, Prager U, Political Mobile Action)
- Liberal/left-wing parents offering "troublemaker training" (e.g., Red, Wine, and Blue; Freedom to Read Project)
- People of color activist groups advancing educational equity (e.g., Black Mamas Matter Alliance, MOBB [Moms of Black Boys], EmbraceRace)
- Parents opposing mask mandates during and after the COVID-19 pandemic (e.g., Let Them Breathe and other anti-mask/anti-vaccine groups)
- Parental groups opposed to racial, gender, and/or sexuality issues being discussed in schools (e.g., Turning Point USA, an ultraconservative group; School Board Watchlist; Citizens for Renewing America—all dedicated to combating critical race theory)

Now, a crucial question: How is a new principal to counter activist parents, considering that these parent groups are influencing district policymakers as well as impacting school and district decision-makers as to what can and cannot be taught in schools? Moreover, these activist parent groups have amassed a coordinated assemblage of school board candidates who push their ideals and from which future like-minded candidates can be recruited.

Returning to the question previously posed: It is definitely difficult, often challenging if not overwhelming, to counter let alone work with certain activist parents due to their highly organized efforts and frequently uncivil, disrespectful behavior. However, all hope is not lost.

Readily consider the "Baker's Dozen" list per Zalaznick (2022). First, an acknowledgment: Activist parental groups are not going away! Zalaznick identifies thirteen noteworthy considerations: (1) Work to forge better relationships by building trust. (2) Do the homework and be prepared to intellectually address education issues. (3) Actively listen and engage parents in decision-making processes. (4) Hold meetings out in the community at places and times that are parent convenient. (5) Spread information to overcome misinformation regarding various school programs. (6) Proactively reach out to families to seek their views as instructional policies and practices are developed. (7) Ensure instructional programs are student-centered and parent-responsive. (8) Establish a strong sense of belonging. (9) Recognize parental perspectives concerning their children's needs (social, emotional, physical, and mental). (10) Monitor social media—expanded digital communication processes have dramatically changed power dynamics and sharpened expectations for student learning. (11) Ensure that all parties (including low-income parents and parents of color) have a voice. (12) Be open and transparent relative to social and emotional learning programs as well as other curricular reforms and innovative instructional initiatives. (13) Maintain open lines of communication.

## Incivility, the Lack of Public Decorum, and Survival Tactics

An emerging force, in the form of a new and different phenomenon, presents a difficult proposition for school leaders, notably new principals. Consider the recent headlines related to parental rights, book bans (most of which are about Black or LGBTQ+ groups), anti-equity initiatives, parent–school board member pledges, and the forceful promotion of extremist local school board candidates. Moreover, the power of teacher unions continues to be threatened, and state legislatures are restricting the freedom of transgender and gender-nonconforming students as well as passing "Don't Say Gay" bills. Additionally, moves are in place, if not already cemented, as to how race and racism are taught in schools (if at all).

Arthur D. Santana, associate professor of journalism at San Diego State University, revealed almost a decade ago (Carroll, 2014) that incivility will be weaponized, and it will serve as a barrier to teaching, learning, and leading. Incivility has become increasingly rampant in schools, where individuals are all too ready to pounce on any particular subject not to their personal liking, often berating educators and other community members both verbally and physically and, in far too many cases, with little or no provocation other than wanting to get their way. And because incivility tactics are so overpowering, users frequently do get their way!

Santana further reports that when a small minority of individuals are shouting, using intimidating, if not vulgar, language—as exemplified in not only school board meetings but also parent-teacher and principal meetings at school—the good, civil people of a learning community, browbeaten and demoralized, become very reluctant to maintain a challenge. Fearing that verbally confronting the harassing opposition, let alone casually speaking to their own side of a discussion, will turn into an all-out quarrel if not an actual fight, civil parents all too often acquiesce to the uncivil opposition.

New principals are often caught in the middle of such frays, where emotions run deep and often out of control, and are more frequently verbally overwhelmed beyond any reasoned ability to think. Planning and/or implementation of what might be intended to best benefit student learning and achievement can be easily disregarded. As a result, teacher well-being, even principal leadership abilities, run the risk of being completely ignored. What is recognized: New principals have purposefully chosen their position in education to aid all members of a learning community so they can contribute to an improved society.

Thus, when new principals find themselves the target of negative feelings and demands—all of which can readily affect their own well-being—they also find themselves inadequately prepared for the battle ahead. These new leaders frequently lack the necessary skills and training to respond, let alone resist.

*New Principal Survival Guide for Success*

Heifetz and Linsky (2002) provide new principals with a "survival guide" for success: Recognize, quickly, when a hostile environment exists, and be sensitive to potential antagonism. Being perceptive and discerning is crucial. New principals must understand and address the underlying reason(s) for animosity and learn to operate above the fracas by being reflective and maintaining a course of goodwill. Such is critical to reducing resistance. New principals must court the uncommitted by recruiting partners, those individuals who will not only stand with a new principal but also point out potentially fatal flaws in any negatively responding strategy or initiative.

New principals must manage conflict, control the potential for destructiveness, and constructively harness the energy of those criticizing or assailing. Additionally, new principals must resist reflex reactions and, even if incensed, respond by being astute, avoiding "cutting off the nose to spite the face." In other words, new principals must be alert, defined, strong, and passionate yet, at the same time, act without animosity and resentment. Not easy!

Heifetz and Linsky continue by noting that new principals can survive by refocusing on the dangers within by knowing their enemies and keeping them close and by managing professional needs with wise actions, remaining at all times student-focused and student-centered. New principals must set an anchor to survive the turbulent seas of leading. New principals must also find a steady and stabilizing "sandbar" from which to secure the "ship" called school by recalibrating their own moral compass and renewing personal and emotional resources. New principals must focus on and distinguish between personal and professional attacks. Most often, the "attackers" are attacking the role, not the person, although that never seems to be the case.

## Technology Redefined: The Age of Digital Leading, Teaching, and Learning—Innovative Today, Obsolete Tomorrow!

Staying ahead of technological obsolescence is and has always been an essential aspect of leading a school. What is new today is suddenly old tomorrow! However, reflect on this Marshall McLuhan (2010) quote: "Obsolescence never meant the end of anything, it is just the beginning." That statement will never be obsolete. As technology in this digital age needs to be redefined, further innovative thinking and processing is the answer. Thinking back or reminiscing is fun, but gains are limited. Futuristic thinking is the key!

That said, recognize that the Radio Shack TRS-80 (1977) was probably the first mass-produced classroom computer, quickly followed by the Apple McIntosh SE/30, the iMac G3, the Dell Inspiron, and the Gateway 2000. Now, here is the fun part: Who in the world of education today has any memory of these hardware devices, all now obsolete? Nevertheless, they were once innovative in design for the classroom or the school's computer lab, at $1,900.00+ each! Thank goodness for futuristic thinking and redefined technology overcoming obsolete hardware and taking the squeeze out of the school's pocketbook!

Finally, technology has readily emerged as an educational force over the last few decades. That said, technology as an emerging force for new principals today must be recognized as neither a bane nor a curse but as a popular and continual educational advancement that creates outstanding learning environments in which teachers convey instruction and students absorb knowledge. Such forces include online learning, distance learning, blended learning, social-emotional learning, mobile learning, personalized learning, project-based learning, and bite-size learning. Also leading the way as an emerging force in education is gamification. New principals must adapt quickly, because students have already done so!

### Social Media Effects

As previously noted, social media, as an emergent force, is a force unto itself! Social media is praised as true connectivity to the world and, in the same breath, decried—if not cursed—as the scourge of society. Increasingly, teachers utilize social media in varied methods as an instructional tool to help students connect with their peers and society and build learning relationships as a means of sharing gained knowledge and expertise and, thus, increasing learning. Yet, there are challenges.

Krutka, Manca, Galvin, Greenhow, Koehler, and Askari (2019) present and address the challenges, if not the problems, of social media and conclude that each must be carefully contemplated and investigated. A seven-point list of social media challenges and problems presented to every new principal is (1) user agreements and how student data is captured and utilized; (2) algorithms of oppression, echo, and extremism; (3) distraction; (4) user choice; (5) harassment and cyberbullying; (6) gatekeeping for accurate as well as inappropriate information; and (7) the digital intersection of curriculum, instruction, media, and learning.

"What's the new principal to do?" Frank and Torphy (2019) recommend, at the very least, that new principals (every principal, for that matter) must be aware, not naïve, of social media influences (both positive and negative); prioritize reasons and resources for social media incorporation; develop technological/digital/social media conceptualizations regarding cause and effect; examine economic and socioeconomic structures related to the use of social media; recognize the ethics shaping social media; and understand said media in terms of how truth, transparency, lies, misinformation, and attacks on democracy relate.

Finally, determine how safe and accurate the medium is. Recall the adage "Buyer beware!" Thoroughly scrutinize what students are exposed to, how such exposure helps or harms, and then make collaborative determinations of usage—when, where, how, why, and for whose benefit. Never be naïve or behind in digital knowledge and social media expertise.

*Note:* Typically, a school district IT department and associated personnel garner these responsibilities. However, such is not necessarily the case in all districts. Bottom line: The burden of responsibility always falls upon the school leader!

## Controversial Issues

Now, more than ever, be aware of and prepared for controversial issues and contentious topics for discussion that will come up in most every classroom—shared either by teachers, students, or both. Such topics include race, racism, gender, religion, racial intolerance, wokeness (co-opted as a pejorative term—that is, expressing a disrespectful meaning or implication), censorship, social order, immigration, democracy vs. autocracy, misinformation, conservatism vs. liberalism—and know that this list is by far not complete!

## Racism and White Superiority in Schools

Regarding controversial issues, a more in-depth analysis is critical. The next topic is not only a controversial one today but also very much a front-burner issue! First, a question: How do schools perpetuate institutionalized racism, specifically in the form of White superiority or supremacy, and how does such operate in the context of education?

Truthfully, racism and White superiority are long-embedded in far too many schools, even today. Such is a result of a long-determined effort—an often unrecognized or ignored controlling methodism—relative to decision-making, curriculum selection, accountability testing, and instructional design and content. All of this is steeped in a long history of Whiteness—a history that is structured as superior to any of the other racial or ethnic groups, particularly those of color.

John Diamond, a professor of sociology and education policy at Brown University, provides a series of perfect examples of institutionalized Whiteness such as those found in day-to-day campus activities, organizational routines, and regular educational practices, such as the starting of school, disciplinary decisions and consequences, grading procedures, the tracking of students, and classroom teacher-student interactions and discussions (Najarro, 2022).

Whether realized or not, sadly if not tragically, White superiority ideals are embedded in far too many individuals' consciousness and self-conscious thinking, incorporating methods that can reproduce a type of racial hierocracy. A few specific and unconscionable examples: Individuals of color are not necessarily as smart; they have a tendency to misbehave more in school; they are much more likely to get in trouble with the legal system; and there is a greater chance they will serve time in prison.

These ideas are not always openly espoused. However, the previous sentence is not an absolute truism, as exemplified in the "Case in Point: Truth Is Stranger Than Fiction—Sometimes Absolutely Beyond Alarming!" textbox. Such ideas are much more likely, especially in education circles, to be either unknowingly accepted or simply inherited practices.

Such practices are sometimes not recognized or propagated but rather are spread innocently, often quietly if not covertly, and readily reproduced when race is not explicitly discussed, studied, and/or related to educational policies, campus initiatives, and/or classroom instruction. Yet, when White educators are asked if such superiority practices could possibly be true, most would earnestly and honestly respond, "Absolutely not! I would not tolerate it!" Or would they?

## "CASE IN POINT: TRUTH IS STRANGER THAN FICTION— SOMETIMES ABSOLUTELY BEYOND ALARMING!"

A White male teacher in a suburban community near Austin, Texas, was initially suspended and subsequently terminated after sharing with a diverse group of middle school students that he believed his race was superior to others. The teacher stated, "Deep down in my heart, I'm ethnocentric, which means I think my race is the superior one." Appearing in a student cell phone video of the classroom incident, the teacher not only made the statement, he appeared in the video to look in the direction of two Black students.

The students in the classroom largely met the teacher's statement with chortles, although some were definitely more subdued. One student, off-camera, challenged the teacher by asking, "So White is better than all?" The teacher then responded with, "Let me finish. I think everybody thinks that. They're just not honest about it."

The teacher continued the conversation, stating, "I think everybody's a racist at that level." One of the Black students responded, "I actually respected you for a while, but now, I don't even have any more respect for you." The teacher then said, "No, you should have more respect because I'm honest." The school principal later shared with the news media, "This interaction does not align with our core beliefs as a district" (Luperon, 2022).

## Pause and Consider

1. Truth is stranger than fiction and, in the following scenario, absolutely beyond alarming. In your opinion, how deep has this mindset permeated schooling and society as a whole? Can you think of other examples in the school setting of which you have seen or heard?
2. What is the meaning of "ethnocentric"? Is "ethnocentric" another term for "racist"? Justify your response.
3. Can such a statement made by the Texas middle school teacher be considered a sign of the times or, from an American perspective, a sign of all times? Defend your response.

*What's a New Principal to Do?*

Professor Diamond further notes that these identified responses are typical yet harmful because each reproduces, repropagates, a type of racial ignorance that permits educators to obscure, misunderstand, misread, or misdiagnose a racial structure that actually exists within schools and society. Other methods of propagation?

Additional examples: (1) child mortality, (2) life expectancy, (3) freedom of societal movement, (4) "stop-and-frisk" procedures, (5) rationalized racial ignorance that simply yet shamefully suggests, "It's okay—those things are not unusual; they're actually normal and, as a result, just happen." Such thinking is more than stinking-thinking! It reveals a complete inability to recognize a societal reality or, at the very least, proliferates an obscurity of that which is being observed (Najarro, 2022).

Where are such breakdowns in schools? Consider race, gender, sexuality, patriarchy—all are root causes integrated, to certain degrees, into regular routines that in actuality serve as school and classroom disrupters. School boards and school administrators, guided by politicians and state laws—if not their own prejudices—dictate that teachers, principals, and students will not talk about race, race history, or critical race theory.

Moreover, teacher voices in far too many states are suppressed relative to voter rights issues; democracy as a societal function; racial equality; racial injustice; social justice; sexuality; trans justice; ongoing book bans; certain societal norms, customs, or traditions; and/or a complete disregard for home languages and cultures. Surely, all beg the ever-present question: "What's a new principal to do?"

Answer: Dismantle racism and White superiority in schools! Next question: How, and by what means? Professor Diamond recommends initiating the following: (1) Diagnose the breakdowns—locate, identify, and eliminate. (2) Redesign the identified breakdowns by ensuring that each becomes less harmful. (3) Hire new personnel. One of the surest methods of bringing change to a school is the selection of newer, younger, and more open-minded personnel. (4) Create induction programs that propagate a non-supremist mentality. (5) Evaluate personnel progress.

Additionally, (6) Engage faculty in racist-deterrent professional development opportunities. (7) Establish racial, equity, and equality coaching processes for advising and retraining teachers and administrators. (8) Connect personnel with roles that are *all* pupil-focused and -driven relative to new and diverse student populations. (9) Advocate against the previously noted efforts to censor or silence on-campus discourse. (10) Create contexts for real, honest, and change-oriented conversations. Each of the ten recommendations must be directed toward racial equality and a non-superiority mentality, as well as other forms of justice for all (Najarro, 2022).

New principals and their teachers must think deeply about (1) personal roles and responsibilities relative to subjectivity regarding race and other forms of inequality; (2) what is being discriminatorily espoused by local, state, and national politicians; and (3) how, as individuals/educators, they may very well see, hear, and even condone such thinking and speech in others and, sadly, often in themselves.

New principals and their teachers must push the narrative of equality and justice for all in public forums, conferences, and conventions, and, most important, recognize when any racial or social injustices are being reinforced in campus routines and classroom actions and activities. At that time, deconstruct and then, properly, reconstruct!

Finally, none of what has been identified or proposed is new, radical, revolutionary, or anti-American. Every written aspect of this chapter segment is about common decency, everyday respect, justice, equity, and equality for all—following the Golden Rule (a tenet of every major world religion): "Do to others as you would have them do to you." In other words, treat everyone as you wish to be treated!

### Now Is the Time!

If new principals have not already noticed, the principalship today is multifaceted, overly demanding, exceedingly difficult, often a pressure cooker, and, as previously noted in chapter 1, a ten-thousand-aspirin job! Has Emergent Force #7: Controversial Issues sent the proverbial "chill up the spine"? Put another way, have controversial issues as an emergent force scared the "bejeebers" out of any new or prospective principal?

Recognize, however, that now is not the time to be timid or afraid, or to panic! Now is the time to understand the controversial issues facing all educational professionals, especially new principals. Now is not the time to idly sit on the sideline and ignore the obvious. Now is the time to step forward and exhibit true leadership. Now is the time to become an advocate for all members of the learning community—now is the time to make a real leadership difference!

## FINAL THOUGHTS

The new principal must be prepared to endure, transcend, and survive the ever-existing, ever-persistent, and ever-changing emerging forces in education, including but not necessarily limited to (1) the pandemic aftereffects;

(2) teacher shortages, quiet quitting, and the Great Resignation; as well as (3) activist parents and school board members. Each force can seriously inhibit a new principal's time, efforts, and ability to lead effectively.

Four additional emerging forces are (4) incivility and lack of public decorum; (5) technology and the age of digital leading, teaching, and learning; (6) social media effects; and (7) controversial issues, again including but not limited to race, racism, gender, religion, racial intolerance, wokeness (as a co-opted pejorative term), censorship, social order, immigration, democracy vs. autocracy, misinformation, conservatism vs. liberalism—a list that can very well go on and on.

Controversial issues arouse strong feelings and can easily divide communities, even learning communities. Issues can arise at any time and will vary from local concerns to national or global matters or alarms. Some controversial issues are relatively noncontentious; others, long-standing. What controversial issues have in common is complexity and highly emotive feelings, and they often serve to create nonrational thinking and discussions.

New principals must be prepared to tackle the controversial issues that create division. While it is tempting to shy away from the obvious, discussing concerns and troubles actually develops important competencies such as breaking down barriers to social interaction, defuses social tension, creates openness to other cultures and beliefs, encourages analytical and critical thought processes, develops flexibility and adaptability when it comes to change, and provides a better understanding and tolerance of ambiguity.

Leading students, faculty, parents, and community members through the complexities of controversial issues is never an easy task for a new principal, but it is one that is often essential, if not critical. Being willing to endure, transcend, and ultimately survive emergent forces exemplifies a competent leader who will bravely labor to bring about an honorable outcome. Remember, rational thinking is far superior to irrational behavior.

## DISCUSSION QUESTIONS

1. Review the section "The Emergent Forces: What Are They? Who Are They? Why Are They?" and share how each force can be a detriment to a new principal. Describe why. Then explain how a new principal can endure, transcend, and survive emerging forces.
2. Examine "The Emergent Forces: What Are They? Who Are They? Why Are They?" again. Which of the seven identified forces have you personally observed a principal encounter? How did the principal handle the emerging situation and force? Would you have handled the situation differently? Explain how and why.

3. Of the seven identified emergent forces, which one, in your estimation, is most critical for a new principal to transcend? Relative to your answer, how and by what means can a new principal prepare, endure, and ultimately survive? Be specific in your response.
4. Has the emergent force of teacher shortages through quiet quitting or the Great Resignation affected your school? How must a new principal handle such emerging controversies? Explain.
5. Activist parents and school board members are forcefully interjecting themselves into curricular and instructional aspects of schooling. Such interjections in themselves are often provocative if not contentious. How can a new principal endure such interpolations, and what must the new leader do to survive?
6. Reflect on the fact that new principals (all principals, for that matter) must lead with civil skills in an uncivil world. In fact, incivility and lack of public decorum are sweeping the nation as emergent forces in all forums, including schools and school systems. Has such reached your school or school system? If yes, how have district leaders handled the issue? Provide examples.
7. Today, controversial issues seem to be more numerous and wide-ranging in communities, schools, politics, and even households. Issues such as racism, race, gender, sexuality, White superiority, and an ever-expanding list of associated topics are pervasive. What controversial issues are compounding leadership in your school? How might a new principal address these issues? Hint: Examine Professor John Diamond's recommendations for a new principal and apply the ten-point tactical method for survival.

## CASE STUDY APPLICATION: STANDING FIRM AND FACING THE FORCE OF THE EMERGING WINDS

This chapter's case study will be applied differently yet significantly. Contemplate Step #2: The Leadership Absolutes Vital to Confidently Experiencing Today's Principalship and, specifically, each of the seven identified emergent forces affecting education today. Next, identify which one of the seven forces has emerged or is emerging at your school. Develop the issue, the circumstance, or the situation into a personalized case study. Next, create a list of either application questions to consider or a series of discussion points to engage other participants. Then present the chronicled information to colleagues in class or to new principals possibly engaged in a book study. Finally, as part of the group interaction, ask fellow contributors how each would face the prevailing winds of the exemplified emerging force.

*Chapter 5*

# Step #3: Learn the Ropes

## *New Principal Expectations, Position Responsibilities, and Skill Sets to Positively Influence New Principal Leadership*

The more the responsibility and expectations on me, the more I like it.
I always love to accept challenges; I get an added inspiration to do better.
Tough challenges always help to bring out the best in me.
(Mushfiqur Rahim "Mr. Dependable," Bangladeshi
cricketer, 2016; QuoteFancy.com, 2022b)

The first responsibility of a leader is to define reality.
The last is to say thank you. In between the leader is a servant.
(Max De Pree, *Called to Serve*, 2001)

The single biggest way to impact an organization is
to focus on leadership skill development.
(John C. Maxwell, bestselling author and speaker,
2007; Antoinette Oglethorpe Ltd., 2022)

### NEW PRINCIPAL EXPECTATIONS: AN IN-DEPTH DESCRIPTION AND EXAMINATION

Expectations can be defined as those strong beliefs, or anticipations, that something will occur. In education, that particularly defined belief or anticipation relates specifically to something happening that is positive, purposeful, goal-oriented, data-determined, student-centered, leadership-driven, and skill-guided. Key expectations for new principals include but are not necessarily limited to the following. The top twenty-five:

- Educate first, administrate second, always exhibiting a relentless focus on teaching and learning.
- Lead, competently and effectively.
- Reveal a student-centered focus.
- Communicate clearly, readily, purposely, and effectively.
- Set goals and learning objectives.
- Develop a shared leadership model.
- Exhibit decisiveness.
- Support teachers.
- Visit classrooms—often!
- Be resilient, persistent, and flexible, and work hard.
- Listen actively—understanding another person's perspective.
- Set high expectations for self and others.
- Exhibit confidence.
- Manage risk and ensure safety.
- Organize and prioritize.
- Empower others.
- Display an even temperament.
- Control student behavior.
- Exhibit empathy.
- Interact through visibility.
- Collaborate and facilitate.
- Manage parents.
- Adapt and innovate (technologically).
- Motivate and inspire.
- Provide guidance and direction.

Another laundry list, but a listing that is crucial, if not critical, for a new principal to accomplish Step #3: Learn the Ropes and thus achieve overall success in gaining teacher support as well as student and parent respect.

## "SIMPLE JOY INSPIRES AND MOTIVATES!"

Following an administrative council meeting, Dr. Norris-Cook, superintendent of Twilligear Marsh School District, turned to one of the district's new principals and asked if she could stay behind for a brief chat. Amelia Harper, new principal at Mueschke Road School, replied positively, and the two began their conversation.

The superintendent asked Principal Harper about the motivational techniques she was applying at her school. Norris-Cook said, "Amelia, I hear good things regarding the way you inspire your faculty. Very impressive for a new principal."

Amelia replied, "It has been quite a learning curve, but one area I think I am pretty good at is being a source for ideas on how to motivate both teachers and staff." Superintendent Norris-Cook then asked the new principal to explain. Listed below is what Principal Harper shared—four stimulating ideas to create campus-wide enthusiasm:

1. Bring simple joy to the team. Determine favorite snacks, songs, and other goodies and then find moments (small or large) to celebrate and treat the team members. A happy faculty makes for a happy principal.
2. Reveal genuine concern and care. Recall the old saying often attributed to Theodore Roosevelt: "Nobody cares how much you know until they know how much you care." Every adult, no matter the age, loves to be loved (platonically, of course). Show care by writing brief notes to faculty. Nothing is more inspiring than receiving a praise note. Something simple like: "Thank you so much for all you do each day for our students. Please know that your dedication does not go unnoticed. Our students and teachers are fortunate to have you on the team!"
3. Recognize faculty. Do so in a campus newsletter, via an email, or publicly. For example: Give a "shout-out" during a faculty meeting. Informally stop by a classroom during a lesson and leave a postcard or even a Post-It note with a caring or inspiring message. And remember faculty birthdays! New principal positivity creates faculty positivity.
4. Everyone has heard of "time-out," so offer something inspiringly different called "time off" and "time added"! Take thirty minutes off a faculty meeting every so often. Do the same with a professional development session. Teachers love "time off." Teachers really love "time added." Add an additional thirty minutes for lunch on professional development days. Take over a class for thirty or forty-five minutes and permit the teacher to leave early. Now, you have motivated the troops, and they will be inspired to give back instructionally!

**Pause and Consider**

1. What have you or your principal done lately to motivate the faculty? Share your ideas.
2. Identify an inspirational technique you have learned from another school leader that has worked very well to motivate faculty and staff.
3. Which of the four motivational/inspirational techniques would you commit to incorporating?

## POSITION RESPONSIBILITIES FOR THE NEW PRINCIPAL

Responsibility—a duty required as a critical aspect of leadership. In education, a principal has a responsibility to ensure the well-being of all campus stakeholders. That particular responsibility is one of many expected to be carried out by the school leader. Key responsibilities of new principals include but are not limited to the following top thirty-five:

- Oversee daily activities and operations.
- Create a safe, secure, and friendly learning environment.
- Establish performance goals and achievement objectives.
- Supervise teachers and staff.
- Plan regular maintenance of school.
- Implement and monitor school policies and regulations.
- Foster a teaching and learning environment.
- Make decisions and solve problems under pressure.
- Develop the campus budget collaboratively with the team.
- Set learning goals based on state and national standards.
- Monitor teacher performance.
- Conduct daily walk-throughs.
- Analyze and present data.
- Research, teach, and model best instructional practices.
- Recruit, interview, select, and hire outstanding school personnel.
- Guide and counsel teachers and staff.
- Manage school emergencies and crises.
- Organize school events, assemblies, and student-centered activities.
- Attend and lead professional development sessions and conferences to gain and share knowledge, expertise, and current educational trends.
- Promote and shape a vision of academic achievement and success for all students.
- Create a positive climate and open culture.

- Develop school leaders from within.
- Improve instruction and curriculum.
- Delegate but never dump.
- Foster change and motivate faculty to change.
- Control the narrative.
- Gain parental support.
- Develop external relations.
- Ensure the well-being of all students and teachers.
- Provide an equity and equality focus.
- Self-reflect; develop a passion for leading, learning, and teaching; and continuously strive for professional growth and development.
- Distribute resources equitably.
- Honor all voices.
- Work to convert pockets of exceptional teaching and learning into schoolwide practices.
- Daily, positively, and effectively impact instructional quality and achievement.

Minute by minute, hour by hour, and day by day recognize the significance of Step #3: Learn the Ropes. By doing so, a new principal can excel with an understanding of personal and professional responsibilities and thus respond with vigor, tenacity, and excellence. First, acknowledge and appreciate the following quote by Vishwas Chavan, inspirational speaker and author: "Self-responsibility, expectations, and accountability are critical to success in personal, professional, and public life. However, we often look for those traits in others, rather than inculcating them in ourselves" (FocusU, 2022).

## The Difference: Expectations vs. Responsibilities

The definitions of the two key terms, "expectations" and "responsibilities," immediately signify a difference. One new principal recently stated, "I'm expected to live up to all administrative expectations and responsibilities! This is what troubles me: What are the expectations and responsibilities? No one has ever provided me with a list, other than my job description."

The new principal went on to say, "During my time in the principal preparation program, I vaguely recall a brief presentation during one segment of one class session, but 'brief' is the operative word. What I need is a handbook listing what is expected of me—the when and where—identifying what specifically my principal expectations and responsibilities are. I continuously feel like I'm flying by the seat of my pants, racing from one dumpster fire to another, always trying to extinguish each before the lids blow off" (Sorenson, 2023)!

Ah, the tales, trials, and tribulations of new principals! Dumpster fires are always ready to ignite and explode. However, the proactive new principal keeps a fire extinguisher ready to damp down any blaze. That "fire extinguisher" is a set of known expectations, responsibilities, and skills—all within quick and easy leadership grasp. The difference between expectations and responsibilities can be viewed as distinguishable within the two paragraphs below:

1. Expectations relate to an action on the part of an individual or individuals who anticipate something to occur or who are looking forward to a particularly helpful activity, event, trait, or skill to be exhibited. Example: The faculty and staff of Ivy Point School expected their new principal to be much like their previous school leader: honest, dependable, resourceful, supportive, and student-focused.
2. Responsibilities relate to a state of being—a principal being accountable, answerable, or even dependable for leadership actions when placed in a position of authority. For example: The director of fiscal accountability telephoned the new principal and revealed that the new school administrator would be responsible for reviewing the campus budget that had been developed the previous year by the previous principal and would need to make a few essential fiscal amendments due to the recent cutbacks in state per-pupil funding.

Responsibilities, expectations, responsibilities, expectations! Living up to both is never simple or necessarily easy—especially for a new principal. Expect this expectation, however: Faculty and staff at the school a new principal is to lead will expect the new leader to live up to their expectations, no ifs, ands, or buts about it! Recognize that, as a new principal, the expectation of their expectation is a land mine set for disappointment and suffering not only for the school leader but also for members of the learning community should said expectations be unfulfilled.

Nevertheless, principal expectations and responsibilities must be faced, met, and ultimately exceeded. Granted, the new principal has minimal control over the expectations of others. Regrettably, that truism does little to alleviate or minimize the expectations and responsibilities of the new principal. Knowing such is more than enough to ensure days of further stress and anxiety. So, what is the remedy? Answer: Incorporate Step #3: Learn the Ropes. As a new school leader, aim for excellence in meeting and exceeding expectations and position responsibilities, and constantly develop a set of skills that will positively influence new principal leadership.

## WHAT SET OF SKILLS POSITIVELY INFLUENCE NEW PRINCIPAL LEADERSHIP?

Previously, in each of the first three chapters, principal leadership skill sets have been identified. For further clarification and application as far as the new principal is concerned, a list of seven key skills that will positively influence new principal leadership are now provided along with further explanation.

### Seven Key Skills to Positively Influence New Principal Leadership

Before examining the key new principal skills, a review of leadership skills is crucial. Skills, characteristics, traits, or talents worthy of repeating include active listening, assertiveness, awareness, intuition, discernment, interpretation, communicative, critical thinking, motivational, compromising, persuasive, and technological. Each of the previously identified skills will readily serve a new principal. Recognize that each skill must be continually honed to a point of near perfection. That is an expectation for which a new principal is responsible! Now, the seven keys to developing new principal leadership skills:

Key Skill #1: *Adaptation*. All aspects of education are constantly changing, advancing, evolving, and innovating. New principals must be responsible for adapting, adjusting, modifying, and altering as required. Flexibility is essential. Such is exemplified in a new principal being confident and adept with the latest in technology. Principals who are unable to adjust and adapt to all aspects of the new digital age can never expect their teachers to gain a serious level of technological competence.

Adapting as a school leader, leading faculty along as well, is simply an expectation—a means of staying ahead of the curve and the students too! Students are very adaptable. They are wired, in fact, to the changes, advances, and marvels of technology! If left behind, a new principal and team will *stay* behind!

Key Skill #2: *Decisiveness*. Being resolute, determined, focused, purposeful, and trustworthy in actions and decisions creates a strong appearance that the leader knows the drill, has the skills, and offers the will to get things done! Additionally, an expectation of principal decisiveness increases faculty confidence in the new leader, which in turn increases the new administrator's own self-confidence.

Key Skill #3: *Equitable, empathetic, and interpersonal*. Sensitivity to others is a very important new principal responsibility. Possessing strong interpersonal skills is an essential expectation of a leader. Students, parents, community members, and faculty will come to school from a variety of backgrounds, ethnicities, religions, and socioeconomic statuses. Like it or not, the world is changing. The country is changing. Schools are changing. Be responsible, and meet the expectation of leading with equity, empathy, and interpersonal skills.

Principals who are not empathetic or equitable in interactions, behaviors, decisions, and reactions will quickly find themselves on a slippery slope to obscurity, if not termination. One final note: Equitable, empathetic, and interpersonal skills relate to possessing the ability to understand and relate to the feelings of others. Empathizing = influencing = leading. Add them all up, and the equation = principal success! An excellent source is the book *Equity, Equality, and Empathy: What Principals Can Do for the Well-Being of the Learning Community* (Sorenson, 2022).

Key Skill #4: *Visible*. Visibility is an open door to an open mind, an open heart, an open welcome. New principals must be seen in the hallways, in the classrooms, in the community, and in the office with the door open, always receptive to interactions with others. Being approachable is all about extending a welcoming hand, showing a desire to recognize, acknowledge, and intermingle and relate with all members of the learning community. A simple expectation of self comes across loud, clear, and concise: "I'm here to serve!"

Key Skill #5: *Endurance*. Look up the word "endurance" in the dictionary. Now, get ready to inwardly smile. Next to the dictionary definition, one might see a photograph of a school principal. It seems the terms "endurance" and "principalship" are interrelated. You cannot have one without the other. Principals endure by being persistent, tenacious, and influential, even during times of hardship, crises, and stressful situations. Remember, endurance is all about being responsible for establishing goals, following routines, pacing, recovering, reaching for support, progressing, choosing a positive "can-do" attitude, having faith, and counting every blessing, one by one.

Key Skill #6: *Self-confidence*. Believing in self and accepting self exemplifies self-confidence. Self-confidence inspires and encourages others to want to believe in their new principal and have a desire to listen and follow. A self-confident leader exudes expertise and creates high levels of trust among followers. Recall the words of former first lady Michelle Obama: "Your success will be determined by your own self-confidence and fortitude" (Bridges, 2017).

Key Skill #7: *Time management*. Time management, as a new principal responsibility, is all about being organized. Being organized helps a principal thrive and achieve on a timely basis. Being time oriented ensures an increase in abilities to plan, strategize, and succeed. Remember, ordinary leaders think merely of spending time. Organized leaders think of using time wisely. Consider reading *The Principal's Guide to Time Management: Instructional Leadership in the Digital Age* (2016).

Seven key leadership skills. Seven methods of succeeding as a new principal. Seven key expectations and responsibilities. Exemplify each of these key skills in daily life and work. Individuals around a new principal will be impressed and, more importantly, impressed with the makings of an outstanding leader!

## THE MAKINGS OF AN OUTSTANDING NEW PRINCIPAL

An outstanding new principal realizes that she or he does not know everything, has a lot to learn, and is confident in one's ability to not only persevere but to achieve, no matter the obstacles. The outstanding new principal leads with a clear vision, has integrity, is honest and trustworthy, possesses strong moral and ethical values and convictions, is humble, helps others reach their goals, takes pride in the accomplishments of others, and never attempts to take personal credit, especially at the expense of others!

An outstanding new principal leads by example; makes the tough decisions; never shies away from solving problems; holds self and others accountable; is courageous and supportive; communicates readily and effectively; develops a passion for leading and learning; is respectful of others, transparent in deeds and actions, and trusting (yet always inspects what is expected); publicly and privately recognizes others; gives credit where credit is due; and loves the school, the faculty and staff, and the students.

Finally, an outstanding new principal realizes how essential it is to:

- Treat teachers as professionals yet hold teachers accountable.
- Ensure that instruction is data-driven.
- Stipulate and expect that students will always be first and foremost in any consideration.
- Welcome parents warmly and friendly, but be recognized as no easy pushover.
- Possess a high level of energy.
- Stipulate and manage good student behavior/discipline.
- Promote team and school—ALWAYS!

- Develop leadership in others.
- Be prepared to serve.
- Hire the best!

Basic responsibilities and fundamental expectations have been identified throughout this chapter. Meeting and exceeding responsibilities and expectations is indicative of what every new principal must aspire to if desiring to learn the ropes and succeed.

## FINAL THOUGHTS

New principals must apply Step #3: Learn the Ropes. Expectations relate to anticipated actions that will be helpful or beneficial to a learning community. Responsibilities relate to a state of being—one of accountability, being dependable or answerable for leadership behaviors and actions.

New principals must be guided by a top twenty-five list of key expectations. Each of these expectations is extremely crucial, if not critical, to overall leader success in gaining teacher support, as well as student and parent respect. Additionally, new principals must be cognizant of a top thirty-five list of position responsibilities to be carried out by school leaders. New principals must recognize that personal and professional expectations and responsibilities are keys to a thriving, flourishing, and productive principalship.

New principals are expected to acquire and master seven key skills that will positively influence their leadership capabilities. These seven skills are adaptation; decisiveness; being equitable, empathetic, and having interpersonal skills; as well as being visible; possessing endurance; revealing self-confidence; and being organized (time management–oriented).

New principals who have the makings of outstanding administrators lead with honesty, integrity, trustworthiness, and a clear vision. They possess strong moral and ethical values and convictions, are humble, aid others in accomplishing goals, take pride in the accomplishments of others, and never attempt to take personal credit. These leaders make tough decisions, problem-solve, hold self and others accountable, are courageous and supportive, communicate readily and effectively, and develop a passion for leading and learning.

New principals who have the makings of outstanding school leaders are respectful of others, are transparent in deeds and actions, inspect what is expected, and love the school, the faculty and staff, and the students. These leaders treat teachers as professionals, are data-driven, place students first and foremost in all decision-making, welcome parents, possess high energy levels, manage student behavior/discipline, promote the team and school, develop leadership in others, serve the learning community, and recruit and select the best.

## DISCUSSION QUESTIONS

1. Step #3 of the seven steps to becoming a successful new principal encourages learning the ropes. In other words, the mastering of new principal expectations and position responsibilities is most essential for any school leader. Of the top twenty-five new principal expectations, which five do you perceive to be the most essential for a new principal's success? Explain why.
2. Examine the top thirty-five position responsibilities of new principals. Which seven responsibilities might be considered the most critical to new principal achievement? Explain the reasoning for those selections.
3. Identify how expectations and responsibilities are alike yet different. Provide a real school example for both.
4. Review the seven key skills for positively influencing new principal leadership success. Of the seven skills, which three skills are most critical in aiding a new principal? Explain why.
5. Think of an outstanding principal you have worked for at some point in your career. What made the principal outstanding, and does your response correspond to any of the descriptors found in "The Makings of an Outstanding New Principal"?

## CASE STUDY APPLICATION: I'M OVERWHELMED— THE EXPECTATIONS ARE CRUSHING, AND THE RESPONSIBILITIES ARE INUNDATING!

Just when the new principal thought things could not get any worse, they did! Today was his twelfth wedding anniversary. Principal Sidney Toler and his wife were scheduled to go out that evening for a nice celebratory dinner. Unfortunately, that plan, like so many others to date, would be interrupted and placed on hold for another day. The problem at hand was more than troublesome, and the new leader was responsible for handling the issue. The expectation was more than just handling the issue. Principal Toler had to resolve the problem.

The new principal thought to himself, *I'm overwhelmed. I'm trying my best to learn the ropes, but the expectations are crushing, and the responsibilities are inundating!* Before recounting the problem, first a setting of the scene: The dismissal bell had sounded earlier that afternoon. It was a beautiful spring day, and students had hurried home to enjoy the warmth before an early-spring cold front pushed through the community. Heavy rain was expected, as was thunder and lightning. Following the students' leaving, the teachers also had plans to get home before the start of the bad weather. *Who could blame them*, thought Principal Toler. *I just wish I was leaving too.*

Now, the problem: That afternoon, not long after the teachers had departed, the cold front came in and with it lots of rain, lightning, and thunder. The new principal was still planning to leave the office to pick up his wife and enjoy a warm and loving dinner, albeit quite wet. Sidney was prepared for the heavy rains, as he had two umbrellas—one in his office and one in his vehicle.

At that moment, the school counselor rang his cell phone. Sidney answered and was asked to come over to the counselor's office immediately. It was urgent! He did so and, upon his arrival at the counselor's office, found the school counselor, Cheyanne Dandler, on the telephone. She quickly motioned for the new principal to close the door and take a seat. Principal Toler did so, still anticipating a brief hello, a what's happening query and response, and then a quick goodbye with a concluding, "I'll take care of it tomorrow." All occurred except the latter. The highly anticipated quick goodbye and "I'll take care of it tomorrow" never happened!

Ms. Dandler, not hanging up, laid the phone down on her desk and said, "Sid, it's an act of God! I picked up my phone to make a call and, low and behold, I could hear Wendy Sheldon (one of the school's teachers) and someone named Leeland DeMace talking. I know this Leeland character is a friend of Wendy's, and she is also a local massage therapist. Now, neither one can hear me, but I can hear them. I've been listening, amongst the heavy thunder and lightning, for more than an hour. I'm telling you, Sid, this has to be the result of the thunderstorm. Why else would such a telephone connection occur?

"They are talking about one of our high-needs students, bad-mouthing our instructional program. They're planning on conferring with the child's parent later this evening and giving her advice and ammunition against us, and they have absolutely no kind words for either you or me. The remarks being made are quite disparaging. I've been documenting it all and already have more than twenty-five pages of notes! Here, read what I have so far; I'll start another notebook."

Principal Sidney Toler, a new administrator, began reading the notes. Page by page, all not only became more and more intriguing but also made the new principal very incensed! The teacher was sharing confidential student information. The new principal also wondered if the teacher was being insubordinate. The new principal took out his cell phone, called his wife, apologized, and canceled the anniversary dinner. This would be another long evening extending well into the night. The school leader then thought to himself, *Why does this have to happen to a new principal?* In fact, Sidney thought, *Why does it have to happen to any principal?*

That night, Principal Toler sat at his computer and contemplated: *Well, things did get worse after all! I'm now so overwhelmed, and the expectations continue to be crushing. Can't I ever get a break? As usual, the responsibilities are inundating!* The principal set those thoughts aside and began reviewing the notes before him, documenting what eventually would become a thirteen-page memorandum directed to the teacher, Wendy Sheldon.

The evidence was consuming. The work of documenting the teacher's transgressions that night was as well. Obviously, what had to occur the next day would be no fun, either. However, the new principal had an expectation to meet and conference with the teacher, as well as a responsibility to proceed with the documentation. He must not only confer with the teacher and share the documentation, but he must also provide due process and ultimately obtain the teacher's signature. The new principal even contemplated an additional series of events, expectations, and responsibilities to include scheduling a meeting with the human resources director, a telephone call to and a meeting with the teacher's labor union representative, and that always aggravating teacher grievance process.

Principal Sidney Toler knew that the personnel issue was a privacy matter, and he would never share the information with anyone except the district personnel director. However, knowing Ms. Sheldon, as he had already learned and experienced, he knew she would not go quietly into the night. Wendy Sheldon would twist her words, documented from her telephone conversation, to best suit herself, then re-twisted, and that story would definitely go against the new principal. Moreover, the teacher's words and associated gossip would spread in a hurry and with great fury!

One thing Principal Toler had learned from this personnel situation was that he must develop a keen sense of awareness in order to identify the supporters and detractors at the campus level. He understood that such would not happen overnight, but this particular night had definitely been a learning experience for the new leader.

## Application Questions

1. Carefully scrutinize the "New Principal Expectations: An In-Depth Description and Examination" section of the chapter. Which key expectations within the top twenty-five list would best serve to aid Principal Sidney Toler as he manages the personnel situation before him? Justify your response.

2. Return to chapter 3 and "The New Principalship: Seven Leadership Absolutes." Which of the seven absolutes identified most aptly relate to the circumstance facing Principal Sidney Toler? Explain the reasoning for your answers.
3. Position responsibilities are listed within the chapter. Review the top thirty-five list. Which of the identified responsibilities best apply to the scenario? Explain why.
4. Survey the following list of expectations and responsibilities that new principal Sidney Toler must live up to as a school leader. Determine which of the items listed is an expectation and which is a responsibility. Support your responses.
   - Schedule a meeting with the district human resources director.
   - Meet with teacher Wendy Sheldon.
   - Share related and applicable documentation.
   - Provide due process.
   - Seek to obtain the teacher's signature relative to the documentation.
   - Meet with the teacher's labor union representative.
   - Prepare for the teacher grievance process.
5. Which of the seven key skill sets identified in the chapter most appropriately apply to Principal Sidney Toler and the case study? Expound.
6. Examine school district board policy specifically as related to personnel. What specific policy relates to this case study? Also, according to board policy, is Wendy Sheldon insubordinate? Explain why or why not. What is due process, and why is it important when disciplining school personnel?
7. Based on the limited information within the case study, how is Principal Sidney Toler on his way to mastering Step #3: Learn the Ropes and thus potentially possessing the qualities of an outstanding new principal? Explain how and why.

*Chapter 6*

# Step #4: Acknowledge and Understand School Norms, Traditions, and Customs

## *What New Principals Must Know to Survive*

Listen, learn, and adapt to the norms imposed.
However, never lose sight of who you are and can become.

I found comfort in challenging the traditions.

I want to be remembered as someone who broke all the customs.
(All quotes unattributed)

### WHAT ARE NORMS, TRADITIONS, AND CUSTOMS FROM A NEW PRINCIPAL PERSPECTIVE? EACH TERM DEFINED, DESCRIBED, AND EXEMPLIFIED

Norms, traditions, and customs. Every school has been blessed or cursed with each—all depending on what they are and what they mean and what good or harm they impose. Also, all depending on who the school leader may be or wishes to be. Consider each of the introductory quotes. One stipulates that a new principal should listen, learn, and adapt to norms imposed. Another suggests that a new principal challenge the traditions. A third recommends that a new principal break all the customs. Question: Which advice presented in the three quotes should new principals take relative to established norms, traditions, and/or customs?

Answer: New principals, in order to survive the school leadership role, would best be served by following Step #4: Acknowledge and Understand School Norms, Traditions, and Customs. But first, a few definitions. What are norms, traditions, and customs? Is each term basically defined as one and the same? Or are the terms somewhat different and, if so, how? The following term definitions are followed by a description as well as a school-related example:

**Norm:**
   *Defined*—Something usual, typical, regular, or routine.
   *Description*—Rules (often unwritten), prescriptive and proscriptive, that are enforced.
   *Example*—The new principal was quite surprised to learn that teachers routinely left campus during conference time to get their hair styled.

**Tradition:**
   *Defined*—A practice, system, or structure.
   *Description*—The fact of a practice being passed on.
   *Example*—The new principal was informed that each week on Friday morning during the fall and before a football game, a school assembly was held in the form of a pep rally. The campus secretary noted, "It's a practice we began years ago. It is nonnegotiable and built into our instructional schedule."

**Custom:**
   *Defined*—An institutional habit, ritual, or pattern.
   *Description*—An accepted aspect, act, or measure associated with doing something specific and relative to a place or time.
   *Example*—The school mascot is an accepted feature at our school, although certain groups find it offensive.

Each norm, tradition, and custom noted above brings to light a dilemma a new principal might face. Each example is fraught with problems, extant or potential. However, some might say, "Right, wrong, or indifferent, that's the way things are done at our school." A question a new principal might initially and privately consider: "Does that actually make it right, or did I lose something in translation?" The dilemma just became an even bigger one. Remember, like it or not, it is a school norm, tradition, or custom. What's a new principal to do?

## What a New Principal Must Know and Understand

New principals will encounter a heavy load of norms, traditions, or customs. One might say that it is normal, traditional, or merely customary. What a new principal must know and understand is that not every norm, tradition, or custom is practical, ethical, or acceptable. Some are, some are not—plain and simple. Listed below are several noteworthy practices for a new principal to incorporate when it comes to determining the acceptability of school norms, traditions, and/or customs.

1. Learn about the campus-wide norm, tradition, or custom.
2. Value and respect the learning community and their reasoning for a certain norm, tradition, or custom.
3. Practice openness, flexibility, and sensitivity.
4. Recognize any personal biases regarding the norm, tradition, or custom.
5. Understand the campus dynamics relative to the norm, tradition, or custom.
6. Determine how said norm, tradition, or custom differs from those of other district schools.
7. Interact with district coordinators, directors, and supervisors if a certain norm, tradition, or custom seems unusual, awkward, offensive, or downright wrong.
8. Adapt to the norm, tradition, or custom, or
9. Make a change. To do so, consider items 10–13.
10. Begin an effort to collaboratively make certain adjustments, revisions, or changes.
11. Ensure positive change or action.
12. Develop into a written rule or regulation any new standard to replace an old, outdated, or problematic norm, tradition, or custom.
13. Accept responsibility for any change to a norm, tradition, or custom.

Knowing, understanding, and often overcoming certain norms, traditions, and customs can make for a complicated new principalship. Schools are people and, much like people, most are set in their ways. When a learning community is set in their way, especially in terms of norms, traditions, and customs, a new principal must remind the team: "Never be afraid to change, even when it is uncomfortable!"

Anne Cohen (2017) extends a clarifying truth when noting that change will happen in life whether anticipated, wanted, or unwanted. She further reminds her readers to be open to modifications to certain norms, traditions, or customs. Altering what is considered by some at school to be sacred can very well be the right thing to do. In truth, instinct often leads not only a school leader but also a team in the right direction. This is known from experience, logic, and even research (Crampton et al., 2018).

## WHICH NORMS, TRADITIONS, OR CUSTOMS ARE INSTITUTIONALLY PERPETUAL? SHOULD THEY BE CHANGED?

Not long ago, a retired school principal shared a funny thing that is not so funny. Writing on a marker board, she reminded her audience of an old-school norm: "No gum." Then she removed the second half of the letter "m" in the word "gum," making the statement read, "No gun." Norms of yesteryear are not necessarily norms, traditions, or customs of this year. Sometimes that's for good; other times that's not the case. When school norms are brought to mind, many think of their days in elementary school: "Be a good neighbor." "Show respect for others and yourself." "Be kind." "Raise your hand before talking." "No running—walk in the hallways."

Those identified norms are good norms. They are built-in traditions or customs that many take into life and share with their own children, whether teachers or not. Other school norms, traditions, and customs, perpetual in nature, may very well need to be changed. If so, what are some examples, and who must be responsible for any change or changes? Identified first are school norms, traditions, or customs that school-age students believe need changing (Sorenson & Goldsmith, 2021).

The kids in their responses, as noted below, were serious, so don't laugh. Okay, feel free to let out a chuckle. Then again, maybe their recommendations need serious reflection. One student stated, "First, the custom of not having a school swimming pool needs to change." Another student shared, "The norm of no talking in the lunchroom is out of date." A third student revealed, "The tradition of one day a week of art class needs to be changed to five days a week." A fourth student added, "My older brother told me that it is a custom for school lunchrooms to have bad food." The sometimes amusing list goes on and on!

Contemplate those institutionally perpetual norms, traditions, and customs, and reflect. Are changes required? Here are some examples:

- Attendance policies.
- Cell phone usage.
- Dress codes.
- Student code of conduct.
- Earlier options for advanced coursework.
- Foreign languages prior to middle school.
- Standards for teachers.
- Improved teaching methods.
- More analytical learning.

- Stronger discipline.
- Greater security.
- Race, ethnicity, and equality training.
- Addressing overcrowding, with fewer portable buildings.
- Equity and diversity.
- Cheerleading, athletics, or other extracurricular activities—more or less?
- Representation gap between principals and students and between teachers and students: Diversity in employees = increased academic outcomes.
- Social issues (poverty; dropouts; homelessness; teen pregnancy and parenting; eating disorders; obesity; child abuse; substance abuse; physical, mental, and emotional abuse; violence; bullying; and suicide).

Should changes in the identified norms, traditions, and/or customs occur? For what reason or purpose? Can the reader identify other institutional norms, traditions, or customs that need to be changed? Who must be responsible for leading change? Four questions worthy of serious contemplation follow.

### How Can a New Principal Make Changes?

First, recognize the significance of Step #4: Acknowledge and Understand School Norms, Traditions, and Customs as related to the change process. According to The Wallace Foundation (2021), new principals can actually effect change in schools, even those norms, traditions, and customs long in need of modification if not transformation. Understand: Principals are the solution; they are the masters of potential change.

For change to be accepted, new principals must attend to strategic cultivation, selection, preparation, and support of a high-quality workforce. Doable? Absolutely! Recall the words of Dr. Theodor Seuss Geisel (1990) in the book *Oh, the Places You'll Go!* "You have brains in your head. You have feet in your shoes. You can steer yourself in any direction you choose" (p. 2).

As previously noted, principals are the key to institutional change when it comes to norms, traditions, and customs. However, principals cannot do the job alone. New principals definitely need to provide support relative to change. However, they too require support from the trenches, the teaching staff.

Acknowledge that four domains of new principal behaviors are critically linked to institutional change: (1) Enhance engagement with instruction, i.e., being instructionally centered, active, supportive, research and best- practice driven, and personally involved in "high-leverage" professional development, instructional meetings, and modeling. (2) Establish a productive and positive climate. (3) Assemble cross-campus leadership teams based on collaboration and facilitation and a fostering of professional learning communities.

(4) Develop effective and strategic management of personnel and resources (human, fiscal, and material).

Specifically, a new principal must be attuned to the establishment of a productive and positive climate as well as an open school culture. A positive climate encourages a supportive, confident, and engaging team as well as a more comfortable, healthy, and enjoyable workplace. An open culture inspires, involves, and connects a school team with one another and with their principal.

## HOW SCHOOL NORMS, TRADITIONS, AND CUSTOMS CAN DICTATE A SCHOOL'S CLIMATE AND CULTURE

Open or closed culture? Positive or negative climate? The choices seem quite reasonable, and an easy determination at first glance. The choices are definitely straightforward. Bottom line: Effective new principals create a climate of a shared vision and positive school goals and expectations and support a strong social, emotional, and behavioral learning environment. Ineffective new principals do just the opposite. Effective new principals create a culture of respect, trust, optimism, and intention. Again, ineffective new principals do the opposite.

Established school norms, traditions, and customs will dictate a school's climate and culture. A new principal can ensure that the school's climate is positive and that the culture is open by recognizing said norms, traditions, and customs and, more importantly, making changes where changes are required. A new principal must set the tone. Stanley Gault, longtime chairman of Rubbermaid and Goodyear Company, once said—and this quote is so applicable to school leaders today when it comes to changing climate and culture—"You have to set the tone and pace, define objectives and strategies, demonstrate through personal example what you expect from others" (Hughes, Ginnett, & Curphy, 2021, p. 114).

Definitions, first. Sorenson (2012) has defined climate as the personality of a school.

- *Climate* influences the behaviors of all stakeholders. It is experienced by faculty and staff, students, parents, and community members, and it is established by the principal.
- A healthy climate provides for meaningful work, motivating challenges, learning opportunities, innovative ideas, instructional/curricular change, creative efforts, goal advancement, and, ultimately, student achievement. Bottom line: A healthy, positive climate stimulates growth and renewal.

- Understand that a positive climate results in effective leadership and competent and caring personnel (Sorenson, Goldsmith, & DeMatthews, 2016).
- *Culture* is a set of beliefs, values, and attitudes shared by all members of a school. New principals must begin to develop an open campus culture by focusing on any one or all of the identified key elements essential to successful change.
- *Establish and maintain high expectations.* Effective new principals, along with teams, hold high expectations concerning student achievement and personnel performance.
- *Provide opportunities for personal growth and development.* Effective new principals, along with teams, attract talented and motivated personnel who strongly desire opportunities for lifelong learning.
- *Develop and utilize personnel policies and regulations.* Effective new principals, along with teams, develop and implement policies that serve to direct instructional programs and ensure compliance with regulatory directives.
- *Establish identifiable decision-making and problem-solving capacities.* Effective new principals, along with teams, meet and make decisions by resolving issues and solving problems via communicative channels, suggestion systems, and research utilization.
- *Create a culture of strong interpersonal relationships and lead with transparency.* Effective new principals recognize that people bring change to people. Clarity, directness, and unambiguousness serve as keys to trust-building. And trust prompts change (Sorenson, Goldsmith, & DeMatthews, 2016).

## How to Change and Improve Culture and Climate

New principals have so much on their plates—so much to get a handle on—just to keep their heads above water. Challenges, obstacles, and detours. It sometimes feels like the Wild West re-created in the principal's office! New principals recognize there is so much to do and learn and so little time. Yes, the work keeps mounting, challenges seldom abating, and there are norms, traditions, and customs to contend with. One well-known area in which new principals must cope with and overcome relates to creating a positive climate and open culture.

Consider the following: A professor at a Southwest university who works with principal interns shares a story of how she can identify, within a minute of walking into an administrative office, the exact climate, if not the culture, of a school. The professor is not clairvoyant, certainly not a psychic, and by no means a teller of fortunes—good or bad.

The professor's theory is based on factual findings, based on what she immediately observes. She reveals that the office staff will readily display a sense of the campus climate and culture. Some schools radiate positiveness, others gloom and doom. The sensory perceptions of the professor are connected, simply, to the initial office personnel greeting, whether it be warm, genuine, and friendly or lacking thereof.

What's a new principal to do if the climate of the school is negative and the culture closed? In other words, a gloom-and-doom school? Positive Action (2022) recommends ten steps to create a positive school climate and open culture:

1. Understand the difference between a positive school climate and an open school culture.
2. Establish a clear vision of expectations, school norms, and goals that will support students, assist teachers, and welcome parents.
3. Ensure school safety is priority 1 from day 1.
4. Advocate for students by assessing if not revising the curriculum and the instructional programs and by showcasing positivity in practice.
5. Promote constructive and optimistic relationships, immediately engaging students, teachers, and parents.
6. Establish boundaries—those guideposts as revealed in student rules and expectations for good behavior. The same holds true for teachers and parents. Guideposts indicative of required expectations and standards for teaching, learning, and positive teacher-to-student and parent-to-teacher behavior must be adhered to by means of defined parameters.
7. Create an atmosphere of fun, not silliness but an environment in which it is okay to laugh, joke, or interact humorously—at no one's personal expense, of course. A happy teaching team, student body, and principal makes for a positive climate.
8. Support and lead professional development by never "dumping" in-service responsibilities on another faculty member—an assistant principal, for example.
9. Promote positive reinforcement strategies.
10. Identify how the campus climate and culture affect student outcomes.

Sorenson (2010, 2012) recommends the following ten important questions that a new principal must carefully consider when attempting to change and improve a school's culture and climate:

1. What does an instructional team value?
2. What attitudes are exhibited across campus?

*Step #4: Acknowledge and Understand School Norms, Traditions, and Customs*

3. What are the mottos, symbols, norms, traditions, or customs of the school, and do they reinforce the main purpose of schooling—students and their achievement?
4. What can or cannot be talked about on campus?
5. How do campus personnel, including the principal, wield power?
6. How do personnel on campus get ahead?
7. How do personnel stay out of trouble?
8. What are the unwritten rules of the school?
9. Do value-based rules permeate the school, and what are those rules?
10. What are the morals and ethics of the faculty and staff, principal included?

Finally, new principals must recognize and understand that culture (climate, too) is a form of currency (Korn Ferry, 2023). Recognize that "two-thirds of the world's most admired companies indicate that 30 percent of their market value stems from culture. One-third revealed 50 percent or more" (Korn Ferry, 2023). Now, pause and think about the television commercial where a Hollywood actor asks, "What's in *your* wallet?" Now consider the question that must be posed to a new principal: "What amount of 'culture currency' is available in your school?"

Is your campus culture and climate exceeding today's market value? In other words, is your school's culture currency indicative of an open or closed culture? Is your school's climate currency positive or negative? If the answer to either question is anything but open and positive, then quickly initiate the ten preceding steps and readily contemplate the ten aforementioned questions. Doing so will aid a new principal and team in moving toward a more encouraging and constructive change. The result can be better than currency in the bank!

## HOW A NEW PRINCIPAL CAN SURVIVE THE CHANGING OF NORMS, TRADITIONS, AND CUSTOMS

Changing the norms, traditions, and customs of a school is all about enhancing and transforming a school's climate and culture. Such change can be positive or negative. However, all change is most often achieved when any one of the following conditions exists:

- *A dramatic crisis*. A shock that undermines the status quo, such as financial setbacks, a serious decrease in student achievement, termination of

a member of the team (including a principal), or, sadly, the death of a team member.
- *A change in leadership.* Anticipate that any new principal will provide an alternate set of values, beliefs, and/or expectations.
- *Young organization.* The younger the personnel of a school, the easier it is for a new principal to communicate and facilitate change. This condition seldom occurs with the arrival of a new principal unless the administrator inherits such a team. Most often a new principal must enhance the campus team with youthful (open-minded) personnel over the course of three to five years (Sorenson & Goldsmith, 2009).

## Changing Norms, Traditions, and Customs by Changing Climate and Culture: Seven Survival Tactics

New principals definitely desire to survive as a school's leader. To do so means making changes—some subtle, others more dramatic. Some changes are handed down by district administration. Other changes are team driven in collaboration with the new principal. Still other changes are principal directed (remember, however, collaboration with team members is always recommended). Listed below are seven methods recommended by Sorenson (2010, 2012) to bring about change that can prove beneficial to a new principal:

1. Ensure that the leadership team serves as positive role models, setting the tone by exhibiting strong ethical and moral behaviors and always leading by exemplary example.
2. Create new norms, traditions, customs, stories, symbols, and/or rituals to replace those currently and negatively affecting the climate and culture of a school.
3. Select, promote, and support personnel who espouse the new values sought and are committed to change.
4. Replace unwritten norms with formal rules and regulations that are readily monitored and reinforced.
5. Shake up current cliques through extensive position rotation or campus transfer. These are drastic personnel moves, but they do work! That noted, principals (new or otherwise) must be cautious about "dumping" a personnel problem on another principal and team.
6. Work to obtain group consensus through the utilization of personnel participation and collaboration in site-based decision-making processes.
7. Last but not least: Create a teaching, learning, and leading environment of high-level trust.

Dr. Zulma Méndez, longtime public school educator and former university professor, once revealed that a positive school climate and an open culture serve as the underlying basis as to why successful schools readily flourish in a change-oriented environment (Sorenson, 2010).

## CAREER LONGEVITY: HERE TODAY, GONE TOMORROW!

The challenge of leading for any principal at any school, at any stage of tenure—new principal or long-term principal—is just that, a challenge! Most new principals understand the cognitive approach to leadership. They realize that leadership is learning, and that learning is a lifelong process. However, the obstacle course and numerous pitfalls the novice principal must "run and leap" are far too often ignored in many university principal preparation programs. Unfortunately, this fact continues to be overlooked at the district level, which fails a new leader when it comes to leadership development opportunities.

Therefore, from the get-go, new principals must avoid the pitfalls that can lead to a career collision or an ultimate career derailment. Noted are five career derailing pitfalls as detailed by Sorenson (2002) for new principals to avoid:

1. The "leaderless" pitfall. New principals must be prepared to accept the responsibilities and expectations associated with the principalship. These school leaders must exhibit a take-charge leadership attitude and recognize when it is appropriate to apply, as the situation demands, the use of any or all of the following: common sense, educational theory, board policy, administrative regulations, and/or education codes. Failure to do so exemplifies the "leaderless" pitfall.

    Each of the noted applications can effectively serve a new principal if incorporated when contemplating how to change a school's norms, traditions, and/or customs that are negatively affecting student progress, teacher instruction, principal leadership, parental insight and involvement, and organizational success.

2. The "indecisive" pitfall. A new principal must be decisive, in command, and exude a high level of self-confidence. These characteristics are not to be confused with arrogance. Indecisive leaders often fail to make necessary, if not essential, decisions related to personnel, problem-solving, planning, establishing a vision, setting goals, building action and improvement plans, and coordinating curriculum with instruction.

3. The "never-seen" pitfall. Visibility, as examined throughout the text, is an essential key to the success of any school administrator. The "never-seen" principal is readily setting themselves up for failure. It is crucial that the new principal be visible and thus send a message to all that they care about the school and stakeholders. Visibility is a surefire method of cultivating goodwill; boosting morale; gathering accurate and timely information; learning about certain norms, traditions, and values; and becoming aware of any potential problems, conflicts, or concerns. President Lyndon B. Johnson once stated, "The best time to make friends is before you need them" (Miller, 1982).
4. The "change when change is not required" pitfall. Granted, the only constant in life is change, yet the novice principal must always be cautious of making changes simply for the sake of change. Rushing to judgment in making a campus-level change can lead to serious repercussions if not carefully thought through with team collaboration.

   It has been said that managers accept the status quo; leaders challenge it! Challenging the status quo simply for the sake of change represents two different articles of clothing. The new principal must know the difference. While easing change into a school is certainly an appropriate and typically effective leadership technique and process, the novice principal must recognize when to act, and then act expediently when change is required. To do otherwise is inviting career derailment.
5. The "uninformed" pitfall. A well-known tidbit of information for the new principal: Leadership involves continuous, organized, individualized, and relevant professional development (Porter & Hezlett, 2023; Sorenson, 2002). Yet nothing is more disappointing to a superintendent of schools or a supervising district administrator than to learn that a new principal is not taking advantage of professional development opportunities. Be the lead learner. Be informed and be a leader who is constantly learning!

## FINAL THOUGHTS

New principals must appreciate and follow Step #4: Acknowledge and Understand School Norms, Traditions, and Customs and be willing to work with or change certain campus norms, traditions, and/or customs. A norm is defined as something that is usual, typical, regular, or routine. A tradition is a practice, system, or structure in place at schools. A custom is a habit, ritual, pattern, or institutional aspect of schooling. Each has a place in schooling, and new principals are apt to encounter these behaviors within a social group.

As a result, knowing how to incorporate the thirteen helpful practices can prove most beneficial.

New principals must recognize that certain norms, traditions, and/or customs are institutionally perpetual and then ask a simple query: "Should these practices be changed?" A list of norms, traditions, and/or customs to contemplate includes but is not limited to attendance policies, cell phone usage, dress codes, standards for teachers, stronger disciplinary techniques, race, ethnicity, equity, and equality.

New principals are provided four behavior domains linked to instituting instructional change: (1) engagement with instruction, (2) establishing a productive and positive climate, (3) building effective collaboration and facilitation capacities with cross-campus teams, and (4) effectively and strategically managing personnel and resources (human, fiscal, and material).

New principals must understand that school norms, traditions, and customs can dictate the climate and culture of a campus. As a result, campus climate and culture may need to be changed or improved. Ten steps to create a positive school climate and an open culture are identified, along with ten important questions a new principal must consider prior to attempting to change or improve a school's climate and culture.

New principals can escape trouble and survive any changing of norms, traditions, and customs by recognizing the causes of most change and then adopting seven survival techniques. Leading is always a challenge and definitely so for new principals faced with the expectations and responsibilities of guiding a learning community. Identified and explored within the chapter are five career-derailing pitfalls that every new principal must avoid: (1) the "leaderless" pitfall, (2) the "indecisive" pitfall, (3) the "never-seen" pitfall, (4) the "change when change is not required" pitfal, and (5) the "uninformed" pitfall.

## DISCUSSION QUESTIONS

1. Review the chapter definitions for norm, tradition, and custom. Consider your school, and provide an observed example for each of the noted terms.
2. Examine the thirteen noteworthy practices to incorporate when determining the acceptability of norms, traditions, and/or customs that a new principal must know and understand. Which four do you perceive to be the most crucial to a new principal's success? Explain why.
3. Contemplate the list of a school's institutionally perpetual norms, traditions, and customs. Which one is most frequently a source of concern for the principal at your school? Identify the reason(s).

4. Study the "How Can a New Principal Make Changes?" section. Note the four domains of principal behavior that are linked to institutional change. Which of the four do you consider to be the most change-centered/oriented? Identify the domain and explain the reasoning for your choice.
5. Explain how school norms, traditions, or customs can drive a school's climate and culture. Justify your response.
6. Which do you perceive to be the most difficult for a new principal to manipulate and/or change, climate or culture? Defend your answer.
7. Review the recommended ten steps to create a positive school climate and open culture. Determine which one of the steps you would consider implementing initially as a new principal. Which last? Explain your reasoning.
8. Reflect on the chapter statement, "A positive school climate and an open culture serve as the underlying basis as to why successful schools readily flourish in a change-oriented environment." Expound as to why Dr. Zulma Méndez is correct in her assessment.
9. Assess which of the five career derailing pitfalls is an absolute in terms of avoidance. Support your answer.

## CASE STUDY APPLICATION: THAT NEST OF HORNETS IS THE REASON THE STINGING IS SO INCESSANT!

### Prologue

Several teachers and a principal met privately one Saturday morning at a coffee shop in a nearby community—far enough from Shermer-Cypresswood School that they wouldn't be recognized. One of the teachers who taught at the school whispered, "I feel like some sort of operative or Cold War spy sneaking around, watching over my shoulder upon entry, and now sitting at this table with my back to the wall!" Others around the table tried to smile but actually revealed more of a concurring grimace.

### The Account

The coffee shop educators began to unravel a story of climate and culture toxicity, one they perceived to be the overriding reason principal and teacher talent was fleeing from Shermer-Cypresswood School: There had long existed what some called a norm, tradition, or custom that was increasingly out of step with other schools and other school districts. These same educators described how new principals became trapped in an organization that was constantly in a downward spiral, whose norms, traditions, and/or customs created a closed culture—both insular and fear-based. For both current and past principals and teachers, negativity had become a drag on curricular innovation, instructional risk-taking, and career satisfaction.

The new principal, as well as teachers and staff, had all been warned not to speak out against district administrators or school board members in any meetings for fear of being ridiculed if not punished or even passed over for any form of promotion. Teachers were reluctant to raise student problems or to speak freely about teaching and learning issues.

Superintendent Ed Rooney had even been accused of giving voice to or providing a sounding board for administrators who acted and sounded like the district leader, often at the expense of being completely non-receptive to difficult messages of truth. The new principal and teaching team members present indicated—cautiously and quietly—that if they spoke out, they might very well be marginalized.

"Agreeability has become the norm, and is more important than capability," said one of the roundtable teachers, quickly noting that she was speaking anonymously. That same teacher explained how she was planning to leave the school after three long years of suffering service. The new principal suggested that some of the leadership team, and far too many teacher coaches, found themselves deep in a culture that failed to face the significant challenges associated with a high level of toxicity, and she believed few saw any possible recourse for positive change.

Another teacher stated emphatically, "That nest of hornets is the reason the stinging is so incessant!" The teacher went on to share, "If a school or school system is so intent on overcoming a toxic work culture, attracting and holding on to the next generation of principals and teachers, it seems to me that the issue of culturally accepted norms, traditions, and customs must be addressed, challenged, and changed."

The current new principal of Shermer-Cypresswood School then spoke: "You know, district leaders and even some of our teachers can talk all day long about instruction, curriculum, accountability standards, and test scores and give lip service as to how wonderful it is to work at our school. But first and foremost, there has to be an addressing of the 'elephant in the room'—specifically, why there is a custom of a closed and toxic culture and a tradition of anything less than a positive climate. Tell me, what can I do?"

## Epilogue

When a school or school system does not want to hear the truth—truth that may very well be bad news—principals and teachers either simply give in and accept the situation or move to another school district. Such does not sit well with new principals, younger teachers, or those tenured teachers who are earnestly concerned about the welfare and well-being of students.

Shermer-Cypresswood School is one in which people do not leave the job; they leave a tradition of toxicity. Campus and school district norms, traditions, and customs matter. How people are treated impacts everything for better or worse. School district leaders and campus principals, alike, must realize that you do not change a tradition of toxicity through emails or memorandums. Positive change comes by developing relationships—listening to and hearing one conversation at a time and then heeding the sound advice offered!

District administrators and school principals, both new and long-term, must show faculty that a students-first mentality and a listening ear to faculty provide for and protect a new norm, tradition, or custom of openness. If a first-rate new principal wishes to create a workplace based on an open culture and positive climate, great talent must be attracted, and it all begins with the new principal leader recognizing the need to eliminate certain norms, traditions, and customs that are institutionally out of step, out of place, and invariably wrong.

## Application Questions

1. First, should a principal ever clandestinely meet with a few members of the teaching staff? Explain why or why not. Does the toxic climate and culture at Shermer-Cypresswood School serve as a condition or an exception for such a meeting? Support your answer.
2. The toxicity of Shermer-Cypresswood School: Can it be most attributed to norms, traditions, or customs, considering each term as defined? Provide an explanation for your response.
3. What one key element could the new principal of Shermer-Cypresswood School most learn from the thirteen practices listed in "What a New Principal Must Know and Understand?" Share your reasoning.
4. Identify methods by which the new principal of Shermer-Cypresswood School could actually make positive changes to overcome the school's toxic environment. *Hint:* See "How Can a New Principal Make Changes?"—specifically, the four domains of principal behaviors linked to institutional change. Which of the four domains is most relevant to the case study scenario? Why?
5. Certainly, the culture at Shermer-Cypresswood School is toxic. Can the high levels of toxicity be reversed? How, and by what means? Review the chapter definition of "culture" and determine which of the five key elements to essential change is most applicable.
6. Reexamine "How a New Principal Can Survive the Changing of Norms, Traditions, and Customs" and "Changing Norms, Traditions, and

Customs by Changing Climate and Culture: Seven Survival Tactics." Which of the change indicators could best aid the new principal at Shermer-Cypresswood School? Focus on two indicators from each subsection. Explain your thinking.

7. What actions, if any, can the new principal at Shermer-Cypresswood School take relative to the district-level climate and culture, specifically as related to the leadership styles/methods utilized by Superintendent Ed Rooney? Is there hope? Can the new principal work around the district's poisonous culture and depressing climate to make improvements at the school-site level? If so, how and by what means? If not, why not?
8. Finally, enlighten as to how the case study scenario relates to Step #4: Acknowledge and Understand School Norms, Traditions, and Customs.

*Chapter 7*

# Step #5: Recognize and Value Essential Characteristics of the Learning Community

## Factors New Principals Must Know and Understand

> A learning community is not based on the knowledge of one expert
> but of many experts working together.
> (Unattributed)

> When principals, teachers, parents, and students
> approach schooling as a community of learners, everyone has
> something to share from which everyone has something to learn.
> This is true collaboration.
> (Unattributed)

### WHAT IS A LEARNING COMMUNITY?

While much has been written about professional learning communities, with serious if not empirical research being conducted in that regard, this chapter will focus strictly on local learning communities (LLCs). However, an astute observer will notice the strong correlation between the two. Specifically, this chapter will place emphasis on who leads the community, as well as ascertain LLC leadership responsibilities. The chapter will focus on identifying members of an LLC and determine essential characteristics of an LLC.

Additionally, the chapter will explore crucial and fundamental factors impacting new principals and learning community relationships, and how new principals must develop a rapport with members of the learning community. The chapter examines key tenets to establishing an effective learning community as well as detailing how a new principal can build a great personal and professional impression. This chapter is all about Step #5: Recognize and Value Essential Characteristics of the Learning Community. The chapter concludes with a review as to how a new principal can learn from failures but ultimately succeed.

What is an exceptional LLC? An LLC is a setting where principal, teachers, students, parents, and community members must share responsibilities for determining academic goals, teaching strategies and techniques, and learning modes and methods. Moreover, an LLC must work collaboratively to create a more consistent curriculum, an enhanced research-based and best-practice instructional setting. Additionally, an LLC must collaborate to develop a campus action or improvement plan designed to establish campus-wide norms and expectations, always reaching for long-term student and organizational success.

An exceptional LLC is a site or setting where shared values, vision, collective learning and applications of learning, and shared teaching and learning practices must be conveyed to best enhance and assess student academic performance. An effective LLC must be designed to focus on student success by means of collaboration, facilitation, relationship building, and collective inquiry. From this point forward, the local learning community will be referred to as a "learning community."

## Who Makes Up the Membership of a Learning Community? Roles and Responsibilities

The roles and responsibilities of members of a learning community evolve around a collective understanding of how all students learn as well as how to ensure increased academic growth and social and emotional development. A learning community is a physical, emotional, and sometimes psychological setting where diverse individuals gather to learn and achieve. While a learning community can be traditionally associated with departments, grade levels, or random groups of faculty, staff, parents, community members, and administration, learning communities are much more.

These members are stakeholders, and they come together in mind and voice to lead lesson studies, conduct action research, initiate team teaching, and seek opportunities to examine and observe, from a campus-wide perspective, the realities of schooling—always extending personal and professional viewpoints beyond the usual and singular classroom vantage point. A learning community is committed to analyzing and prioritizing goals, objectives, and student data as well as concentrating on teaching enhancements and student improvements.

Members of a learning community typically include but are not limited to the following:

- *Principal.* The principal shapes a vision of academic success for all students, creates a culture and climate amenable to effective teaching and essential learning, develops leadership capabilities in others, analyzes data to improve instruction, offers and leads professional development, models best-practice instruction, and manages school personnel and resources.
- *Instructional coaches* aid teachers and students in skills development, academic goal setting, learning strategies, time management, organization, study habits, self-regulation, and self-efficacy, as well as improving social and emotional behaviors—all to enhance academic success.
- *Teachers* provide a variety of learning opportunities, instructional materials, and educational resources for use in learning activities. Teachers observe and evaluate student progress, development, and performance. They assign and grade course work, homework, tests, projects, and other learning endeavors.
- *Students'* voice is gained and heard to better contribute a greater perspective relative to curricular and instructional decision-making. Students participate in learning activities, engage in cooperative learning, obey teachers, maintain good behavior, become organized, manage time on tasks, exhibit good study habits, and abide by school and classroom rules.
- *Parents* demonstrate interest in and remain informed regarding their children's progress, as well as offer ideas, suggestions, and recommendations in appropriate settings (i.e., parent forums, question-and-answer sessions with principal and teachers), and engage in site-based decision-making committees. Moreover, parents offer important suggestions, recommendations, and outside perspectives at learning community sessions. Parent responsibilities include supporting the school's rules and disciplinary consequences, being involved in teacher-parent conferences, and following the advice of school staff in how to assist with their child's learning and behaviors.
- *Community members* are often defined or described as those individuals who live, learn, work, play, and pray in communities. Community members may have a formal leadership role (mayor, police chief, rabbi or minister, businessperson, retired educator, etc.) or may simply be friends and neighbors, often with grown children no longer attending school in a district, who are recognized as individuals who are natural leaders and are thus apt to be "movers and shakers who get things done."

Community members may engage in curricular and instructional decision-making; participate in forums designed to improve student achievement, behavior, and well-being; and offer guidance to a principal and faculty as a means of better understanding community issues, problems, values, traditions, language(s), and cultural actions and behaviors.

Community members may also offer support for innovation in curriculum implementation and instructional programs, assist students in on- and off-campus learning, aid and support teachers, provide safe havens for students, and offer information that reveals a valuing of students, including student safety and security.

- *District administrators* offer educational support, guidance, direction, and leadership as requested or required. District administrators assist, always in collaboration with campus leaders and faculty, with the development, implementation, and evaluation of curriculum and instruction as well as school district and campus policies, procedures, and regulations.
- *Others* include outside consultants and educational experts whose role is to aid school and school district personnel in managing instructional change, solve curricular issues, offer advice and expertise, and improve numerous aspects of performance.

## Position Responsibilities for the New Principal: A Learning Community Member

The term "responsibilities" has been defined as (1) a duty that is required and (2) a critical aspect of leading. Responsibilities are accepted obligations with correlated accountabilities. The principal's role as a member of the learning community includes those responsibilities and expectations previously noted in chapter 5.

Those position responsibilities are now further expanded to include seven additional descriptors: (1) analyzing and reviewing of student data; (2) establishment of learning goals with SMART (Specific, Measurable, Achievable, Relevant, Time-Bound) objectives; (3) inclusion of up-to-date research-based best-teaching practices; (4) regular scrutiny of campus resources (human, fiscal, and material) to better ensure the facilitation of new teaching practices, curriculum development and renewal, and innovative instructional programing; (5) consistent planning for and application of student-centered learning activities; (6) advancement of student academic performance; and (7) organizational success—all within a safe and secure environment.

The principalship is an important position with decades of research conclusively recognizing the principal as the most important and influential role and position at a school. Yet the position, in terms of importance, is always relative, frequently taken for granted, and sometimes, unfortunately, disparaged—all depending on who is being asked about the role and position.

## Position Importance Is Relative: It All Depends on Who You Ask!

A new principal comes into the leadership role with a strong sense of purpose and pride, along with a desire to work toward a vision and associated goals that will build essential skills in self and in others, all designed to enable the school year to progress smoothly. Not only does a sense of purpose serve as a career driver, but so does a sense of importance—within reason, of course. Are the noted descriptors naïve or realistic? The answer to that question all depends on who is asked. Reflect on the following scenario. Then answer the Pause and Consider questions that follow.

### CANNIBALS AT SCHOOL!

Recently, a school system hired several cannibals, which was quite unusual but necessary considering the shortage of personnel available to schools in need.

"You are all a part of our team, now," said the personnel director at the new employee orientation session. "You will receive all the usual benefits, and you can go to the school cafeteria for something to eat during your thirty-minute lunch period, but do not eat any of the faculty and staff members." The cannibals promised they would not.

Six weeks later, at a follow-up new employee professional development session, the personnel director remarked, "You all are working very hard, and I am most satisfied with your efforts. However, the school secretary and two custodians have disappeared, and you know how important these individuals are to our organization. Do any of you know what has happened to these fine people?" The cannibals all shook their head no.

After the personnel director departed, the cannibals' team leader loudly exclaimed, "Which one of you idiots ate the secretary and the two custodians?"

Two hands rose reluctantly, to which the cannibals' team leader responded, "You fools, we're in trouble now! We've been eating the school administrators for six weeks, and no one has noticed!"

Source: Based on an old joke frequently titled and told as "Cannibals in the Workplace."

**Pause and Consider**

1. The "Cannibals at School!" scenario serves to humorously remind new principals who the most important adults at a school are, as perceived by or whom asked? Who are these most important individuals, and why is the campus principal not at the top of the list of most important school personnel, at least in the scenario? Is there a reality to the story? If so, explain. If not, why not?
2. How is a new principal to best ensure they are the most important adult at school without becoming egotistical or arrogant in the process? What specifically does a new principal need to do to earn the "title" of most respected, admired, and important?
3. In an effective learning community, is it important that a group doing the greater good be considered the most important individuals on campus? Who might be the group doing the greater good and why? What greater good is this particular group doing? Explain.

## WHAT ARE ESSENTIAL CHARACTERISTICS OF A LEARNING COMMUNITY?

Step #5: Recognize and Value Essential Characteristics of the Learning Community is all about acknowledging that the best learning communities are those strongly supported by the school administration. They are collaborative in words and actions, and they establish a common vision and mission, as well as value experimentation. The best learning communities craft and maintain—through faculty development—relevant and doable goals; ensure inclusive, not exclusive, membership; and serve as a model for building relationships, again through collaboration and facilitation. Such learning communities exhibit positive attitudes and strong work habits. They share expertise and react and respond with a time-sensitive, intense action mentality.

The best, most-effective learning communities are distinguishable by seven essential characteristics: (1) a shared mission, vision, and student-centered goal orientation; (2) a collaborative team effort that is focused on student learning and achievement; (3) a collective inquiry (teams fostering shared knowledge and thus learning together and from one another); (4) an action-research and experimentation focus whereby teams are never afraid to try different tactics, approaches, and/or methods, and are always willing to take risks; (5) a commitment to continuous improvement; (6) an effects orientation and results emphasis; and (7) a principal who exhibits strong leadership and always offers support and encouragement.

## How Do Certain Crucial and Fundamental Factors Impact a New Principal's Relationship with a Learning Community?

Fundamental factors are defined as those basic yet essential principal-centered leadership functions that influence and contribute to positive results or outcomes. First, what are these fundamental factors? Second, how do they impact or influence a new principal's relationship with a learning community? Grissom, Egalite, and Lindsay (2021) emphasize the following four factors. New principals are responsible for:

- Factor 1: Engaging instructionally with teachers.
  - Impact: Principal importance and influence on instruction, teachers, students, and learning cannot be overstated. Principals *are* the most important individual at a school. That importance bears heavily, especially on new principals. Such a weight can be positive or negative. To impact the learning community, new principals must have a serious and significant instructional background and must be prepared to exercise that knowledge and competency with vigor and expertise.
- Factor 2: Establishing a positive campus climate and open school culture.
  - Impact: Climate and culture, as previously examined in chapter 6, are developed and influenced by the new principal in partnership with faculty and staff to effectively establish a learning community environment marked by trust, efficacy, teamwork, data analysis, active engagement, and continuous improvement.
- Factor 3: Facilitating productive collaboration.
  - Impact: New principals aid and promote strategies of collaboration, which in turn influence teachers to work together better, both authentically and dependably. New principals must always facilitate the advancement of supportive improvements in practice, while collaborating with teachers to enhance student learning and achievement.
- Factor 4: Managing resources (human, fiscal, and material) strategically.
  - Impact: New principals develop strategic practices in hiring the very best teachers and staff and allocating fiscal resources to better ensure that teachers and students have the necessary supplies, materials, technologies, and facilities from which to learn and achieve.

## DEVELOPING A RAPPORT AND ESTABLISHING A RELATIONSHIP WITHIN A LEARNING COMMUNITY

Will (2019) recommends the most effective methods or elements essential to developing a connection and establishing a relationship with a learning community. It is critical for a new principal to initiate five essential elements—and not engage in five corrosive undertakings.

1. **Do** achieve teacher buy-in and commitment. Any change at school, especially when accepting a new principal, is a difficult prospect, to say the least. Teachers, parents, and students need time to acclimate (adapt, adjust, and familiarize) themselves with the new personality. A principal change has the potential to sour teacher relationships with the leader, or with any newly proposed programs or initiatives. New principals must provide everyone the time necessary to commit to the change in leadership.

    **Don't** immediately begin making changes. If a new principal wants buy-in from faculty, the wrong way to achieve such support is to announce, "We're going to make these changes, now!" Chances are, that short statement with lengthy implications just dampened the potential for a positive initial teacher-principal relationship.

2. **Do** continue to work with what is already working. Everyone recognizes the adage "If it ain't broke, don't fix it!" The same can be applied to schooling. Now, recognize that change will come, but remember that with such change, it is essential to maintain certain successful elements that have been working and later incorporate said elements into any new program or initiative.

    **Don't** ignore veteran teachers. Yes, some of the "old pros" are cynical and really need to move on, but most veteran teachers have years of practice, experience, and advice that will be very beneficial to a new principal. Heed their counsel and lean on the very best.

3. **Do** build relationships. Trust is the most effective and reliable method of building faculty respect and relationships. Be honest, fair, dependable, trustworthy, respectful, and supportive and you'll watch person-to-person relationships grow and flourish.

    **Don't** be conceited or arrogant. An egotistical know-it-all is anything but respected; fill in the blank with an appropriate mocking "anything" term: Mr./Ms. _____.

4. **Do** become highly visible. Get out of the office. Walk the hallways. Stroll into the classrooms. Talk with everyone—students, teachers, paraprofessionals, custodians, groundskeepers, maintenance repair

personnel, and, definitely, parents. The new principal will learn much by being out and about. Do office paperwork before or after hours.

**Don't** ignore suggestions or recommendations from faculty and staff while visibly being available. One of the first orders of business for any new principal is to be an active listener when making the rounds. Every member of the learning community has a lot to share, some good and some bad, but everyone needs an opportunity for an honest, respectful conversation and, definitely, to be heard. Granted, some conversations will be anything but respectful, but those individuals generally need to be heard too. Suggestions and recommendations will come in abundance, but all can ultimately be waded through by incorporating visibility, time, and good judgment.

5. **Do** pilot new initiatives before arbitrarily making nonnegotiable changes. If change is mandated by state education code or district requirement, pilot the new initiative (change) first, if at all possible. Members of any learning community find a piloted program much easier to swallow than a program that's shoved down their throats. "Pilot" means just that—guide, lead, try, experiment, test, practice, and review.

**Don't** arrive unprepared. Recall the old song "Don't come to the dance floor, cowboy, if you forgot to wear your boots!" Bottom line: New principals must come to school prepared. Get ready, get set, GO!

## FIVE KEY TENETS CENTRAL TO A NEW PRINCIPAL ESTABLISHING AN EFFECTIVE LEARNING COMMUNITY AND BUILDING A GREAT PERSONAL AND PROFESSIONAL FIRST IMPRESSION

New principals must establish an effective learning community by developing great personal and professional first impressions. Such impressions are the result of inclusion of five key or central tenets. New principals must:

1. *Actively communicate* and take every opportunity to engage with others, including teachers, students, parents, community members, and district office administrators. Stay out of the office during school hours. Be out and about conversing—in classrooms, milling areas, out on the practice field, in the band hall or choir room. Be seen, be engaging, and be there! An initial positive impression will be made, and building a strong and effective learning community will begin through strong communicative efforts.
2. *Be open and accessible*, always personable and approachable. As noted in chapter 1, maintain an open-door policy. Welcome comments

and constructive criticism, and be prepared for an occasional negative comment. They go with the territory, and eventually a thick skin will develop! Members of the learning community will quickly realize that even though you are a "green" prospect, you are there to actively listen and readily respond. A second positive impression will be created.

3. *Learn quickly*—very quickly—the names of all faculty and staff. Attempt to place names with faces, if possible, before the faces of individuals arrive for the start of a new school year. Acknowledge people by name when they first come to school to meet their new principal. After the start of the school year, begin—again very quickly—learning the names of students. Always acknowledge as many students as possible by name, pronouncing each correctly. A third positive impression.

Everyone appreciates being called by name, and everyone loves it when they are known by name before they think that will occur. Recall the theme song of the classic television show *Cheers*:

Sometimes you want to go/Where everybody knows your name/And they're always glad you came./You want to be where you can see/Our troubles are all the same./You want to be where everybody knows your name (Portnoy & Hart-Angelo, 1983)

4. *Accept questions*—even when you have no idea of the answers. Actually, a new principal already knows the answer to every unanswerable question that will be posed: "I don't know the answer to that question, but I'll get an answer for you before the day is over." Then, do so! A fourth positive impression.
5. *Answer questions.* Always bring back a response to every inquiry made. Teachers, parents, students, community members—all have an abundance of questions, and they all want answers. Make cell phone notes or simply jot down a note the old-fashioned way, with a pen and pocket notebook. Doing so ensures that you will not forget to get an answer to a query. Now, an answer to an individual's question has been provided and a final positive impression has been made.

## How New Principals Fail but Succeed

Mistakes will happen. They are not uncommon during a principal's first year as a school leader. When a mistake occurs, admit it; never cover up a mistake! Obscuring, suppressing, or conspiring to cover up a mistake is a critical mistake. Maxwell Maltz (onetime leading self-image expert) said, "You make mistakes. Mistakes don't make you." Albert Einstein (theoretical physicist) noted, "Forget the mistake. Remember the lesson." Denis Waitley

(American motivational speaker) suggested that "the only person who never makes a mistake is the person who never does anything" (QuotesCover.com, 2012–2021). Finally, Edna St. Vincent Millay (American lyrical poet) wrote, "I am glad that I paid so little attention to good advice; had I abided by it I might have been saved from some of my valuable mistakes" (QuotesCover.com, 2012–2021).

When new principals make a mistake, they often fail, and when they do fail, they can actually begin to succeed. Peter Economy (2022) and Sorenson, Goldsmith, and DeMatthews (2016) share the 7 Bs to overcoming failure in order to succeed:

1. *Be helpful.* Aid the learning community through difficult times and experiences. Lessons can be learned from mistakes and failures and then turned into successes.
2. *Be supportive.* Risking failure is much more palatable if the new principal is encouraging others to take risks, even though there may be uncertain results. Acts of courage must be supported, not punished.
3. *Be willing.* Talk about mistakes and failures. Discussing mistakes is learning, not failing. Openly talk with members of the learning community at regular intervals about how academic projects are progressing, what risks are being assumed, how success is around the corner, and how failure—when it does occur—is only one aspect of life that can often lead to success or, at the very least, to a lesson learned.
4. *Be honest.* Trustworthiness and forthrightness are two characteristics of strong new principals. If a mistake is made, don't soft-pedal it. Be honest, speak the truth, and admit the mistake.
5. *Be timely.* Learn to project good timing. When is the right time to begin a new instructional project or program? When is a proper time to initiate an instructional change? Excellent questions to consider. Remember, bad timing leads to bad problems. Errors happen; mistakes are made. Complexity follows uncertainty. Dysfunction becomes failure. Timing. Yes, it is all about timing!
6. *Be watchful,* especially for potential pitfalls. Recognize that pitfalls or traps are often laid by leaders themselves. One of the most frequent self-laid traps of a new school leader is being labeled "lazy," "incompetent," or "difficult." Such labels can not only destroy learning community relationships but also erode potential and positive change (Jordan, 2022). Be careful, be watchful, and sidestep those ever-lurking pitfalls. (Review the chapter 6 section titled "Career Longevity: Here Today, Gone Tomorrow!".)
7. *Be resilient.* Mistakes can and will slow down a leader's progress, leadership abilities, and even reputation. Mistakes will happen. Failures

will occur. The best leaders never let either get them down. Bounce back, try again, move on, learn lessons, experiment again, but keep on keeping on.

## Remember This, Not That!

Now, a moment of truth and transparency: Yes, at times new principals will find leading a school to be more than challenging. Try overwhelming! In all honesty, such is the principalship for most new school leaders. That said, what can be learned before wading into the deep end or taking that long walk off a short pier? The new principal must be sensitive to and keenly aware of what is important and what is not. In other words, remember this, and don't do that! See table 7.1.

**TABLE 7.1 Remember This; Don't Do That!**

| Remember This | Don't Do That |
| --- | --- |
| Offer kindness. Be mindful of the feelings of others. | Lead self and not others. Leading is serving others, not self. |
| Respect others. Value others in words, tone, gestures, and written communiqués. | Know everything. Know-it-all people are not liked. Be open to advice and learning. |
| Extend patience. Planning, projects, and changes take time. Set reasonable expectations. | Ignore a mentor's advice. Successful leaders seek out the wisdom of others. |
| Extend humor. Laughter is often the best medicine. Judicious humor makes work enjoyable. | Fail to be gracious. Treat everyone with respect. Recognize contributions. Extend appreciation. |
| Provide truthfulness. Deliver truth, always. Be candid but never mean, petty, or harsh. | Neglect to support others. Everyone wants to succeed. Lend a helping hand. |
| Be encouraging. Lift others. Recognize strengths, skills, and contributions. | Be angry or resentful. Never take it personally. Let go; forgive and forget. |
| Offer gratitude. "Thank you" are two of the most pleasing words in the English language. Use them frequently. | Lie, gossip, or lack integrity. Integrity breeds success. A lack of integrity is a leader's ruin. |
| Convey hope. Hope is seeing the light at the end of the tunnel. Lead faculty to recognize things will get better. | Expect perfection. High standards, yes. Quality, yes. Remember, perfection does not exist. |

Sources: Kevin Daum, Inc.com (2022), "8 Critical Things Every Great Leader Remembers"; Caren Merrick, carenmerrick.com (2020), "10 Things Highly Successful Leaders Must Forget and Never Do"; A. S. Mungal & R. D. Sorenson (2020), *Steps to Success: What Successful Principals Do Every Day*, Rowman & Littlefield.

## FINAL THOUGHTS

New principals appreciate and actually profit from Step #5: Recognize and Value Essential Characteristics of the Learning Community. New principals understand what a learning community is, who makes up the membership of a learning community, and what the learning community membership responsibilities are. New principals seek to understand how certain crucial and fundamental factors impact a new principal's relationship with a learning community and how to develop a rapport and establish a relationship within a learning community.

New principals must initiate five essential elements and not engage in five corrosive undertakings. New principals must know what to do and not to do. Five key tenets central to a new principal establishing an effective learning community and building a great personal first impression are identified. The chapter details how new principals can fail yet succeed (including the 7 Bs to overcoming failure in order to succeed). Finally, new principals are provided with guidance in terms of "Remember this, and don't do that."

## DISCUSSION QUESTIONS

1. What is a new principal's role and responsibility in service as a member of the learning community? Why is the principal role important, if not essential?
2. Identify the essential characteristics of a learning community. What factors impact a new principal's relationship with a learning community? Of the four factors identified, which one do you perceive is most critical from a new principal's perspective? Clarify your response.
3. Examine the "Do and Don't" segment of the chapter. Which of the "Do" items might be considered the most important for a new principal to develop when establishing a relationship with learning community members? Explain.
4. Inspect the five tenets central to a new principal establishing an effective learning community. Of the five tenets, which two could prove most beneficial to a new principal in establishing an effective learning community? Describe why. Of the two selected, which one might best create a positive first impression for a new principal? Detail why.
5. Reflect upon the 7 Bs to a new principal overcoming failure in order to succeed. Which three do you believe are the most important to a new principal in overcoming failure in order to succeed? Expound on your response.

6. Review table 7.1: Remember This; Don't Do That! Of the eight "remember this" items, which three must a new principal be keenly aware of? Justify your answer. Of the eight "don't do that" items, which three could be the quickest ending to a new principal's once-promising career? Rationalize your responses.

## CASE STUDY APPLICATION: HE DOESN'T HAVE ENOUGH SENSE TO COME IN OUT OF THE RAIN! OR, HOW NOT TO BUILD A RELATIONSHIP WITH THE LEARNING COMMUNITY

Vernon Astoria began his first principalship at George Feeny School a little over two months ago. This was Vernon's first principalship, and he knew he would do well because he believed in doing things by the book, as well as by "his way or the highway." Vernon Astoria was the type of man that seldom took good advice, even when it was great advice and handed to him on a silver platter. He was simply accustomed to doing things on his own and doing it as he thought best.

Recently, one of the veteran teachers at George Feeny School had heard from another teacher at the school where Vernon Astoria had been an assistant principal. The teacher from the other school said, "Mr. Astoria couldn't lead himself out of a burlap sack if he had the directions inside with him and the top wasn't tied!" The veteran teacher listened but figured such was just talk from someone full of sour grapes.

The veteran teacher, Alice Sue Landers, stopped by the office of Principal Astoria a few weeks later in hopes of providing him with some sound advice regarding communication. The principal had corresponded with the teachers regarding a new mathematics program he was mandating. He had described the program as nonnegotiable and, as noted in his email, "You teachers need to get with the program and start implementation immediately!" Alice Sue Landers was well respected by the school's other teachers, as well as students and parents. She was a very knowledgeable and caring math teacher and thought she would share a few tidbits that might help the principal with the tone of his email communiqués.

Her visit with the new principal did not go well. When Alice Sue Landers offered her first suggestion, the principal exploded and said, "Mind your own business. Do as you are told!" The veteran teacher was stunned and humiliated. Later, in private, she shared the following with one of her confidants, another team member: "He called me on the carpet. I was dumbfounded, quite disturbed. I hurriedly told Mr. Astoria 'Yes, sir' and walked out of his office."

The murmurings regarding the new principal and his tacky remarks had started well before Alice Sue Landers went to offer him communication advice. Other teachers were already snickering behind the principal's back, calling him "Mr. Know-It-All." Alice Sue Landers tried to stay above the fray and remain professional, especially when disrespectful names were being bandied about. But one day, when she had experienced enough, she let slip a statement that would become the teaching staff's mantra when referencing Principal Vernon Astoria: "No doubt, he's won the really incompetent boss lottery!"

Day after day, week after week, the "lottery-winning incompetent boss," as he continued to be referenced, worked to dismantle previous curricular and programmatic structures, further alienating faculty and staff. Additionally, he mostly remained behind closed doors, only venturing out on occasion to berate his secretary, Faith Corvatch, or let loose on some unsuspecting teacher who happened to be in the office.

The school's assistant principal was new in her role, as were the two instructional coaches. All toed the line and jumped when Mr. Astoria said "jump," as they constantly feared retribution. Soon teachers began to speak of transferring to other schools, even before Christmas break. Two teachers resigned at midterm, saying, "We've had enough of 'Mr. Know-It-All.' Because of our husbands' salaries, we can move on and simply stay at home. A good rest, after working for this principal, will do us good!"

Other teachers were not so fortunate. Many even filed grievances and, as a result, were either overtly or covertly harassed by the school leader. Still, Principal Astoria remained. The veteran mathematics teacher, Alice Sue Landers, told a large group of teachers one morning while everyone was sitting in the workroom before the start of school, "Ladies, we can do this. I've outlasted other principals—granted, not as bad as this one—but we can outlast Vernon Astoria. We all know he doesn't have enough sense to come in out of the rain!"

The teachers laughed, hugged one another, and agreed that they too could outlast their leader. As the teachers quickly exited the workroom for class, one said, "Sad, isn't it. We all thought it would be good to work with a new, young, energetic principal. Boy, were we wrong!"

## Application Questions

1. It has been noted within the chapter that position importance is relative. Explain how Principal Vernon Astoria is important in his position as school leader and how he is unimportant. Provide examples to support your conclusions regarding the principal's relativity.

2. Does the learning community at George Feeny School meet any of the criteria relative to essential characteristics of a learning community? Why or why not? Why has Principal Astoria been unable to have a crucial and fundamental impact in building a relationship with the learning community? Explain; include examples.
3. Examine the five key tenets central to a new principal establishing an effective learning community. Focus on how Principal Astoria is not building a great personal or professional first impression. Of the five tenets, where is the principal most deficient? Explain why. Of the five tenets, what must the new principal do to gain the respect and acceptance of the learning community? Or is it too late? Provide a detailed explanation.
4. Study table 7.1: Remember This; Don't Do That! Which of the "remember this" items can be attributed to new principal Vernon Astoria? Which of the "don't do that" items can be attributed to the new principal?

*Chapter 8*

# Step #6: Appreciate and Incorporate Policies, Regulations, and Procedures

## New Principal Legal Responsibilities

> We have to follow the law.
> We don't have a choice in this matter.
> (Michael Polzin, national pharmacy store executive, QuoteHD.com, 2022)

> No man is above the law and no man is below it:
> Nor do we ask any man's permission when we ask him to obey it.
> (Theodore Roosevelt, twenty-sixth president of the
> United States, AZQuotes.com, 2022b)

### WHY ALL THE LEGALESE?

Recently, a student arrived early for her Educational Law class and sat visiting with the course professor. She shared that she and her husband had binge-watched a streamed television series about crime and criminals. The student exclaimed to the professor, "I want the criminals in that show brought to justice. I want the law applied!" The professor, who has also been captivated by the program, replied, "Well, you know it is a series; I actually stayed up late last night and watched the final show. Do you want to know what happens?" The student smiled and asked, "Is the law applied? I just want justice. No, don't tell me. I'll watch later tonight, after class, and see for myself!"

Laws are made to be obeyed. It is human nature to desire that justice be applied to those who disobey the rule of law. When legal disobedience occurs, there is actually a longing that all be made right. Dwight D. Eisenhower, supreme allied commander during World War II and, later, thirty-fourth president of the United States, once stated, "The clearest way to show what the rule of law means to us in everyday life is to recall what has happened when there is no rule of law" (BrainyQuote.com, 2022a). His reference was to the tyrannical fascist and authoritarian regimes of the 1930s and 1940s.

Yet, dare we admit a reality? Sometimes we do not necessarily believe that the law applies to us. Think for a minute: Did you speed today? If you did, you broke the law—a law that applies to you and everyone else. If caught, many are quite aggravated; there is a ticket and fine involved, and insurance rates may increase. As humans, we sometimes want it both ways: the laws applied, yes; to me, no! When it comes to schooling, there are laws, and these legalities apply to teachers, principals, and district administrators. New principals must recognize and utilize Step #6: Appreciate and Incorporate Policies, Regulations, and Procedures, because the legal responsibilities associated with the principalship are not to be taken lightly.

## NEW PRINCIPAL LEGAL RESPONSIBILITIES

These educational laws come in the form of state and federal codes, school board policies, administrative regulations, and campus procedures. Failure to obey these laws results in a consequence. Sometimes the consequence is simply a slap on the wrist; other times, a written reprimand. Still other times, the result is more serious consequences, including but not limited to lawsuits, civil monetary penalties, termination, and, potentially, revoked credentials—even incarceration. Read the following scenarios and respond to the Pause and Consider questions that follow.

## ROMANCE AND FINANCE—SCENARIO #1

Ray Walter and Jim Cross, two professors, were team-teaching a principal-preparation course when a graduate student seeking her administrator's certificate asked a straightforward question: "Can you tell us how new principals sometimes find themselves in legal jeopardy?" Dr. Walter responded first, saying, "Easy—the two most common ways involve either sex or money!" The students laughed. Dr. Cross then replied, "Humorous, yes, but the truth is that romance and finance are the typical methods by which principals, new or tenured, find themselves in legal trouble."

The two professors went on to share a couple examples with the students. Dr. Ray Walter, who had served numerous years as a superintendent of schools, referenced a finance-related superintendent example that occurred in a Southwest school system. Dr. Jim Cross, a longtime university professor of education, revealed another criminal example—this one romance-related—stating, "Let's call it what it is: sex in the workplace." Identified below are two real-life examples.

Example #1: Romance (sex). A new high school principal decided to go into the office one Saturday morning to catch up on some paperwork. The one-building school district was located in a rural community, and the principal noticed that the superintendent's and business manager's cars were parked outside the district offices.

When the principal entered the building, he noticed that the superintendent's office door was slightly ajar with the lights on. The business manager's office door was closed. The principal thought to himself, *Great minds think alike. We are all here catching up on work.* He then walked down the corridor to his office.

After working for a little more than an hour, the principal decided to grab a cup of coffee and go into the superintendent's office for a chat. Pushing the superintendent's door open, to his great surprise and embarrassed disbelief he found the business manager and superintendent in a very compromising position—on top of the desk!

The most heartbreaking aspect of the compromising situation was that the district business manager was the high school principal's wife, and she had been having an in-office rendezvous every Saturday with the superintendent of schools. Both the superintendent of schools and the business manager were soon terminated. The high school principal quickly resigned due to the humiliation associated with his wife's indiscretion and moved to another school district. Truth is stranger than fiction!

## Pause and Consider

1. How could one surmise that the "romance" scenario was a legal predicament?
2. What does school board policy stipulate relative to sexual activity on campus between school personnel? For more information regarding school board policy, read the next section.
3. In what ways could the behavior of the superintendent and business manager affect the climate and culture of the learning community?

## ROMANCE AND FINANCE—SCENARIO #2

Example #2: Finance (money). The superintendent of an urban Southwest school district conspired to defraud the school system by securing a $450,000 sole-source contract under false pretenses. The scheme also helped the superintendent earn an additional $60,000 in school district bonus funding (Fernandez, 2013).

The superintendent was subsequently arrested at his office, handcuffed, marched past a large group of teachers and principals engaged in a professional development session, and then escorted by Federal Bureau of Investigation agents to a federal courthouse. There the superintendent was charged with conspiracy to commit mail fraud and aiding and abetting theft from instructional programs receiving federal funds.

Charges for one of the country's worst education scandals called for up to twenty years of imprisonment in a federal facility. The superintendent resigned in disgrace to await federal prosecution and sentencing. The superintendent had all education certificates revoked, ultimately served a much reduced 3.5-year sentence in a federal prison, and was last heard to be working for a roofing company in a major city across the state. The scenario proves the old adage, "Crime doesn't pay!"

## Pause and Consider

1. What specific school board policy relates to this scenario?
2. Letitia James, New York attorney general, stated, "No matter how powerful or political one might be, no one is above the law" (*ABC News*, 2022). Whether in the twentieth century (see the Theodore Roosevelt introductory quote) or during the twenty-first century, there will always be individuals who are (a) corrupt and (b) believe they are above the law, much like the superintendent in the scenario. Research the scenario and determine how and by what means the superintendent's original sentencing was so significantly reduced. Provide an explanation.
3. Two questions: Is the sentence and time served fair? Why or why not? Was the superintendent above the law? If yes, how was such possible? If not, explain your reasoning.

## SCHOOL BOARD POLICIES

Both scenarios show that every new principal must know the rules—the laws, codes, policies, regulations, and procedures—or suffer the consequences.

What are school board policies, and how do they apply to new principals and members of the learning community? First, schools and school systems function in a complex environment of legalities. The United States has long been a litigious country. Schools are a microcosm of American society and, as such, face litigation on a regular basis.

The question to consider is how does a new principal avoid legal entanglements? The US Supreme Court has long ruled that teachers, principals, and other school district administrators can be held personally liable for fiscal damages for violating the constitutional rights of students. New principals must therefore be legally literate and know, understand, and apply school board policies.

## What Are School Board Policies?

School board policies serve as written statements of decisions, principles, guidelines, or courses of action related to the guidance and governance by which a district and schools within a district must operate. School board policies reflect essential authority directives sanctioning programs, personnel, and services and specifically outlining a new principal's implementation of each.

Policies also define school purposes and prescribe a framework within which all administrators discharge their assigned duties. Policies define intents, requirements, implementation, and the administration of education code. Policies are the "how" districts and schools are to operate legally. Bottom line: School board policies are legally binding guidelines specifically designed to ensure that new principals—and all school personnel—remain trouble-free when it comes to the law.

Sorenson and Goldsmith (2009), in the classic and bestselling text *The Principal's Guide to Managing School Personnel*, relate that on any given day, a new principal can be faced with a barrage of issues, complications, and problems—some of which may very well involve the potential for legal entanglements. During the course of a single school week, a new principal may deal with considerations based on the law, such as:

- Copyright
- Appraisals of performance
- Communicable diseases
- Hiring
- Absences
- Inappropriate internet activities
- Sexual harassment
- Disciplinary action, sanctions, and/or appeals
- Academic freedom

- Employee assistance programs
- Confidentiality and right-to-privacy issues
- Intoxication
- Alcohol and drug testing
- Grievances
- Suspensions and dismissals of employees
- Arrests and convictions

New or prospective principals who are taken aback by this listing must seriously consider Step #6: Appreciate and Incorporate Policies, Regulations, and Procedures and recognize how critical new principal legal responsibilities are to the effective functioning of a school. Complying with school board policies promotes intelligent decision-making and most certainly serves to ensure that new principals remain free of legal entanglements.

## School Board Policies and New Principal Responsibilities

New principal responsibilities are clearly identified and defined by school board policy, as are those for all school personnel. New principal responsibilities are defined in school board policy as "duties." For example, most school board policy manuals across the nation stipulate that the principal shall:

1. Assume administrative responsibility and instructional leadership in accordance with the rules and regulations of the school board and be directed by the superintendent for planning, management, operation, and evaluation of the school's educational program.
2. Submit recommendations to the superintendent of schools regarding the appointment, assignment, promotion, transfer, and dismissal of all personnel assigned to the school.
3. Assume administrative responsibility for all records and reports required regarding pupils, transfer of pupils within the school system, and promotion of pupils.
4. Have the authority to discipline students up to and including suspension from school or from a school bus, as provided for in the Code of Student Conduct (TASB.org, 2022).

This list is an example of how school board policy identifies, guides, and clarifies new principal duties.

A major section of any board policy manual specifically relates to school personnel. This section of the policy manual is quite significant, not only for personnel but also for principals who must manage personnel. The school board policy manual guides and directs principals relative to personnel duties, expectations, and principal-related personnel responsibilities. When graduate students in university principal-preparation programs are asked what aspect of schooling principals are apt to find the greatest chance of legal entanglement, the answer, time and time again, is "special education." Good guess, but a wrong answer! The correct reply is "school personnel."

New principal responsibilities can be overwhelming. Guidance and direction by school board policies cannot be underestimated. Finally, new principals must recognize that without board policies, a school district would cease to function, as good policies relate to good business in education (Sorenson & Goldsmith, 2009). The very best new principals study the district's policy manual and clarify with district administrators how policy is developed, adopted, and implemented.

## ADMINISTRATIVE REGULATIONS

Statements as to how school board policy is to be applied and implemented by principals and district administrators are typically referred to as administrative regulations. Such regulations may be reviewed by school boards for compliance with education code (the law) and board policy. Regulations are typically left to administrative discretion in both design and implementation.

Administrative regulations define how policy is to be executed. An administrative regulation can designate a management process; specify how policy is to be enforced; provide direction and instruction; give examples in the form of exhibits, forms, and/or management reference tools; provide specific application of policy; and/or expand or complement school board policy.

## CAMPUS PROCEDURES

Campus procedures are defined as school-based practices, measures, methods, or, simply, ways of doing things while on campus. Campus procedures are identified as those actions generally related to but not necessarily limited to school personnel. Examples include but are not limited to the following:

- Teacher times for reporting to school as well as departing from school
- Teachers departing school during a conference period or at lunchtime
- Library attendance times
- Times for students to engage in art, music, physical education classes, etc.
- Use of paraprofessionals (instructional aides)
- Material Center usage and check-in/checkout procedures

- Campus bell schedule (when classes begin/end)
- Scheduled dates, times, and frequency counselors are in the classrooms
- Master schedule development and implementation
- Identification of other procedures as implemented on campus

## FINAL THOUGHTS

New principals have legal responsibilities to follow state and federal education codes, school board policies, administrative regulations, and campus procedures. Failure to comply with these legalities results in consequences. School board policies are specific written statements of decisions, principles, guidelines, or courses of action related to the guidance and governance by which school district administrators and campus faculty and staff must operate and abide.

New principals must recognize that Step #6: Appreciate and Incorporate Policies, Regulations, and Procedures serves to define educational purposes and prescribe a framework within which all administrators discharge their assigned duties and responsibilities. The policies themselves prescribe intent, requirements, implementations, and administration of education code. Policies are the "how" school districts and schools must legally operate.

New principals face a barrage of issues, complications, and problems on a daily basis. Some of these concerns may very well involve the potential for legal entanglements. Therefore, new principal duties and responsibilities are clearly identified and defined by school board policy. In fact, a major section of any school board policy manual relates specifically to school personnel. Policy directs principals relative to personnel duties, expectations, and principal-related personnel responsibilities.

New principals must understand the differences between school board policies and administrative regulations. The latter are statements as to how school board policy is applied and implemented by principals and district administrators. Regulations are frequently left to administrative discretion in both design and implementation. For example, administrative regulations can designate a management process, specify how policy is regulated, provide direction and instruction, and give examples in the manner of exhibits, forms, and/or management reference tools. Regulations also provide specific application of policy and/or expand or complement school board policy.

New principals are expected to recognize and institute campus procedures, which are actions typically related to teacher and staff expectations. A few examples: (1) What are teacher times for reporting to school as well as departing from school? (2) May teachers depart from school during a conference or period or at lunchtime? (3) What are the procedures for developing

*Step #6: Appreciate and Incorporate Policies, Regulations, and Procedures* 125

and implementing the master schedule? (4) What are the established library attendance times?

New principals must commit to school board policies, comply with administrative regulations, and institute campus procedures. Each serves to provide guidance and direction for principals, teachers, and staff members. Just as important, policies, regulations, and procedures better ensure that new principals and school personnel remain unhampered and unburdened when it comes to legal entanglements.

## DISCUSSION QUESTIONS

1. Define the purpose of school board policies. Provide an example as identified within your school board policy manual.
2. Describe the intent of administrative regulations. Offer an example as instituted within your school district.
3. Explain the reasoning for campus procedures. Advance an example from your school. Justify why the identified procedure is important to the functioning of school.
4. What does your school board policy stipulate when it comes to romance and finance issues in schools? Identify three personnel-related school board policies, and detail why these policies are essential for ensuring legal entanglements are minimized.
5. Review "Romance and Finance—Scenario #2" and reconsider, first, the introductory quote by Theodore Roosevelt and then the Scenario #2 quote by New York attorney general Letitia James. Now seriously contemplate this question: Is no man above the law no matter how powerful or political? A second relatable question: Does the query provide a truthful perspective or merely extend a deceitfulness that is designed to subvert reality and provide a false hope to the average law-abiding citizen? Support your responses.
6. Explain why all the legalese and why it is essential for new principals to understand, implement, and abide by the law (education code and board policies).

## CASE STUDY APPLICATION: YES, I HEARD WHAT HE SAID. BUT HE SAID HE FOLLOWED SCHOOL BOARD POLICY!

For a variety of reasons, the head coach was upset with certain female members of the athletic department coaching staff. Whether the reasons for irritation and aggravation were legitimate or not was a question for another day. What was most significant this day was what the head coach had said, not necessarily why he had said it. Head Coach Bob Curtin had shared with the male coaches his frustration with the female coaches by stating:

> "I'm going to slit their throats, slide them down the bank, and let them float down the river and bleed a slow death!"

The statement, while made in reference to some of the female coaching staff, was greeted by the male coaches with cautionary responses. One coach, James Cody, was married to one of the female coaches Bob Curtin had referenced. Head Coach Curtin did not realize that Coach Patricia McCormick was James Cody's wife. Coach McCormick had retained her maiden name after recently marrying Coach Cody. James Cody went home after the meeting and reported all to his wife.

School networking is phenomenal, and it did not take long for Patricia McCormick to contact good friend and fellow female coach Freda C. Dobbs. Well, that was all it took; soon the grapevine was full for the picking, with call after call from one female coach to another. Freda C. Dobbs took great offense at Head Coach Bob Curtin's comments and immediately called her new principal, Norman Newman, who seemed a bit befuddled but finally retorted, "I think that's probably not the thing for the head coach to be saying."

Coach Dobbs replied sarcastically, "Oh, really, you think not?" Then she seriously asked, "What do you think should be done?"

The new principal stumbled a bit and then said, "Let me check board policy."

Coach Dobbs curtly replied, "Well, Mr. Newman, you do just that. I'm calling the district personnel office and reporting the statement made by Head Coach Curtin; then I'm going to the district offices and file a grievance against him. Now, you go ahead and check that board policy!"

Soon an avalanche of calls began rolling into the district personnel office. Later, all eight female coaches would meet with a personnel officer and file grievances against the head coach. The dam had been broken. One female coach after another was bound and determined to see the grievance process through. One of the male coaches, a strong supporter of Bob Curtin, defended the head coach to the director of school personnel, saying, "Yes, I heard what he said. But Coach Curtin told me he had followed board policy! Coach Curtin also shared with me that he didn't use or say any of the female coaches' names. Plus, he said he was just joking!"

Step #6: Appreciate and Incorporate Policies, Regulations, and Procedures 127

## Application Questions

***Important note:*** Utilize local school board policy to assist in responding to the following questions.

1. How does Step #6: Appreciate and Incorporate Policies, Regulations, and Procedures relate to the case study scenario? Provide one or more examples.
2. "He didn't use or say any of the female coaches' names. Plus, he said he was just joking!" Are these good reasons for the filed grievances to be ignored? Not using names and "just joking": Do the noted excuses provide any or sufficient protection by school board policy? Are the excuses sufficient reason to dismiss the eight grievances?
3. What does your school board policy stipulate about speech at school? Consider what Head Coach Bob Curtin said and determine if such statements are "true threats" or "offensive or harassing speech."
4. Do the words spoken by Head Coach Bob Curtin constitute a "hostile work environment"? Explain why or why not.
5. Coach Freda C. Dobbs plans on suing Head Coach Bob Curtin as well as the new principal and the school district on the basis that the statements made by Bob Curtin are defamatory (remarks damaging the good reputation of someone; remarks that are slanderous [i.e., insulting, malicious] or libelous [i.e., unfounded, vilifying]). Could the spoken words be considered defamatory statements, specifically if the law assumes that an individual's reputation has been injured? Could the school district be sued? The head coach? How about the new principal, Norman Newman?
6. Are there other legal complications or potential entanglements?
7. What can be said about the new principal, Norman Newman? What aspects of the chapter could be applied to the new school leader and why? Does the new principal have any responsibility (legal or otherwise) or recourse relative to this particular situation?

*Chapter 9*

# Step #7: Enhance Personal Attributes Critical to a New Principal's Success

## The Leadership Protocol

> Always be ready to explore both positive and negative traits by evaluating self!
> (Dr. Prem Jagvasi, speaker, trainer, and leadership coach, GoogleQuotes.com, 2022a)

> Self-evaluation helps guide thoughts, emotions, and behaviors—all in a healthy direction!
> (Anonymous)

### DIRECTIONS

This inventory has been developed as a means of acknowledging the significance of Step #7: Enhance Personal Attributes Critical to a New Principal's Success. The leadership protocol will take approximately fifteen minutes to complete. Examine each of the eight statements and imagine yourself, as a new principal, in each of the scenarios. Enter answer A, B, or C in the blanks provided. Each answer should most closely match your likely response as well as your leadership style and associated traits and aptitudes (skills).

The "likely" response is generally the first answer (A, B, or C) that comes to mind. It is essential that you respond to each statement accurately and honestly. Scoring interpretations will follow the statements and the multiple answers presented.

1. A special community meeting is being held in the school auditorium to debate key educational issues. As a new principal, you decide to make a difference and . . .
   - A. Chair the meeting, lead discussions, and respond to questions.
   - B. Remain thoughtful, considerate, and cautious in speaking to personal views.
   - C. Take minutes and later transcribe them into a community newsletter.
2. You receive a telephone call in the middle of the night from a parent you counseled in your office yesterday. The parent's abusive husband is once again threatening her life and that of her child. The parent and child have sought refuge in a hotel, scared and weighing options. As a new principal, you are certainly concerned for her emotional and physical safety. You decide to . . .
   - A. Call the police on her behalf, insist she press charges, and then provide her with the name and number of a lawyer who will aid her in obtaining a restraining order.
   - B. Make necessary arrangements for her to meet with school counselors as well as an outside agency as a means of helping her with a series of next moves.
   - C. Grab your car keys and drive directly to the hotel with your female school counselor to better ensure the parent's safety and well-being.
3. While visiting with your school mentor in your office, you confide how much you are overwhelmed with way too much on your plate. You are not ready to step down as new principal, but you . . .
   - A. Come back to reality and realize there is a light at the end of the dark tunnel. You walk out of the office, go directly into a classroom, and become reenergized, ready to lead with greater vigor.
   - B. Tell your mentor after an hour-long conversation that you could always go back to being an assistant principal, knowing a job opening is available at a school in a neighboring district.
   - C. Decide the visit with the mentor was one of value, and grasp how difficult it would be for the school and school district to have such an imposition placed upon all. It's best to bear up and meet the challenges.
4. The director of curriculum and instruction for the school district has been terminated due to unethical, if not immoral, behaviors. Although a new principal, you decide to . . .
   - A. Use the ongoing weekly administrative council meetings and luncheons to interact with the key district "movers and shakers" to secure the insider track for the position.

*Step #7: Enhance Personal Attributes Critical to a New Principal's Success* 131

   B. Volunteer to serve as interim and ask to be considered for the position.
   C. Bypass the headache of an opportunity and stay on as a new principal, finding ways to make your contributions stand out so that the superintendent views you as a team player and district asset and possibly promotes you at a later date.
5. Since you have recently moved to the school district as a new principal, you hope to develop new professional relationships with key district players and local community leaders. To engage with these individuals, you . . .
   A. Watch and learn who the movers and shakers are and work to leverage your professional network to best benefit your career goals and advancements.
   B. Join and volunteer at one of the local service clubs as a means of getting to know community leaders and build a reputation as a solid worker, problem-solver, and consensus-builder.
   C. Box up some items for charity, take them to a local shelter, and ask how you may continue to be of assistance.
6. The superintendent of the school district states that he believes in delegating responsibilities to principals. The superintendent wishes to incorporate you, as a new principal, into this form of leadership. From your perspective, the superintendent seems to be "dumping" a large amount of work and responsibilities on you, creating long work hours into the night and on weekends. You . . .
   A. Document your added responsibilities and workload as part of an ever-expanding résumé and hope to gain an even greater role and better position in a nearby school system.
   B. Wonder how long the superintendent expects you to continue with the expanded work and responsibilities, as you believe the demands are infringing on your own productivity as a new principal, not to mention placing a hardship upon your family.
   C. Ask that the superintendent stop by the school office for a cup of coffee, and share with him, "I arrive at school each day by 6:00 a.m. and over the past four to five weeks have rarely departed the office before 10:00 p.m." Additionally, you share, "I need to know if this is your expectation of me as part of the principalship so I can decide if it is something I want to continue for the long term." Then you ask this question: "Just for a point of clarification, are you grooming me for another role or opportunity within the school district?"

7. The district maintenance department grounds crew recently did a less than acceptable job relative to groundskeeping. You are now considering . . .
    A. Calling both the maintenance director and the superintendent of schools and letting both know that the finished work is anything but complete and far from acceptable. You request that the crew return to the campus first thing tomorrow.
    B. Getting the word out to the other principals that the grounds crew did shoddy work and ask if they have experienced the same problems. If so, what do they recommend that you do?
    C. Taking matters into your own hands and spending all day Saturday at school with your personal lawn equipment to ensure that the job is done correctly.
8. Parents on campus with young families have asked to use the facilities (a couple of unoccupied rooms) to set up a volunteer-led day-care center while the parents do volunteer work on campus. You . . .
    A. Immediately agree to make the space available.
    B. Explain to the parents that you will have to research the feasibility of such a venture.
    C. Review school board policy and then seek district approval to ensure that the facility can become a reality.

## SCORING

Add up the responses you have made with an A answer. (For example, of the eight statements presented, five have been responded to with an A answer.)
The total number of A answers = \_\_\_\_\_.
The total number of B answers = \_\_\_\_\_.
The total number of C answers = \_\_\_\_\_.

## SCORING INTERPRETATIONS

### Mostly A answers: Driven

- Natural leader with high standards for self and others.
- High-energy.
- Exceptional communicator.
- Goal-oriented and achievement-focused.
- Directly influences issues.
- Unambivalent.

- Mantra: "I can make it happen!"

**Mostly B answers: Diplomatic**

- Creates relationships.
- Natural intuitive leader.
- Motivates circle of influence.
- Uses terms such as "we," "us," and "let's."
- Collaborates for rewarding outcomes.
- Problem-solver and decision-maker.
- Rarely seeks center of attention.
- Personal sense of responsibility.
- Gives and garners loyalty and respect.
- Mantra: "Let's make it happen together!"

**Mostly C answers: Dedicated**

- Creates concepts and visions.
- Facilitator.
- Demanding work ethic.
- Eager to help others.
- Highly competent and quality-oriented.
- Hands-on and innovative.
- Reliable team player.
- Hard worker (possibly a workaholic).
- Perfecting and involved in every detail.
- Mantra: "I can help make it happen!"

**You are a combination of two or more of the A, B, and C answers.**

- Not unusual at all. Many people are a combination of each of the indicators.
- Exhibits different styles of influence, leadership, and aptitudes in different circumstances.
- Powered by all three leadership profile indicators: driven, diplomatic, and dedicated.
- Mantra: "I can be a high-octane mover and shaker, depending on the situation!"

Research has long shown that most new principals exhibit different styles of leadership, traits, and key aptitudes (skills) at different times, all depending on the situation (Blank, Weitzel, & Green, 1990; Fernandez & Vecchio, 1997;

Hersey & Blanchard, 1977). You very likely fit into this particular category, though such is not an absolute. Some new principals are **driven**, others are more **diplomatic**, and some are simply **dedicated** servants; yet most new principals are a **combination** of any two or all three of the leadership profile indicators.

Does one of the four noted areas of leadership styles, traits, and aptitudes rank higher and make a new principal a better leader? Not necessarily! The very best principals, new or tenured, frequently make decisions and solve problems either as driven leaders, skilled diplomats, or dedicated servants—again, all depending on the situation.

Source: Adapted in part from C. McIntosh, "What's Your Power Style?" (2006).

## FINAL THOUGHTS

The old farmhouse can be seen in the distance, more than fifty yards away from a weathered barn. Attached to the barn door is a rugged, cast-iron ring. Off the back porch of the farmhouse is another attachment: a second worn ring, firmly fastened to the door frame of the old homeplace. Both rings, securely affixed to their respective buildings, serve to uphold a lifeline during harsh winter blizzards. From each ring, a rope can be attached so the resident farmer can take essential steps from one building to the other, never losing mental sight of his destination, yet keeping a tight grip on the rope and taking careful strides into the depths of deepening snow. The line ensures that the farmer's steps will not go awry during a blinding snowstorm.

The use of a safety line reminds the new principal of the need to take careful but essential steps to gain vital skills and realize the key expectations required of a new leader. School leadership can often present new principals with "blinding snowstorms"—those times when a significant gain is in the often-unseen distance. A guiding line is required to get from one place to another, one goal to the next, one decision to a problem solved. That guiding line, which offers essential step-by-step directions, is *Essentials for New Principals: Seven Steps to Becoming Successful—Key Expectations and Skills*.

So, new principal, grab the rope line (this text) and follow the required seven steps. Use the text and the seven steps to overcome the new principal leadership storms. Each step is necessary to generate eventual administrative success. A firm grasp of essential skills and key expectations will lead the new principal along a path of great promise. Now, lead on, new leader!

## EPILOGUE: BE AWARE, BE PREPARED, NEVER DESPAIR, AND LET YOUR LIGHT SHINE

New principals have much on their plates, and often it seems that new principals find themselves spinning each of the plates—running from one plate to the other, trying to ensure that the plates continue to spin and don't fall and break. Such can be overwhelming, if not despair inducing. As a concluding message to new principals: Always be aware, be prepared, never despair, and let your light shine. Sometimes that's easier said than done. However, new principals must:

*Be aware* of such social issues as—
- Civic education
- Race
- Gender
- Religion
- Cultural differences
- Immigration

*Be prepared* to overcome—
- Political polarization
- Nationalism
- Racial intolerance
- Censorship
- Cultural restraints
- Misinformation
- Anti-democracy tendencies

*Never despair*—
- Recognize and remember the following quote attributed to George Washington:

  We must never despair; our situation has been compromising before, and it has changed for the better; so, I trust it will again. If difficulties arise, we must put forth a new exertion and proportion our efforts to the exigencies of the times. (Quotefancy.com, 2022a)

*Shine your light*—
- Especially on those students, faculty, parents, and/or community members who are experiencing difficulties in life.
- Recognize a widely held tenet of many world faiths: Let your light shine before others, that they may see your good deeds.
- Be moral, ethical, and legal in all actions and behaviors.
- Be kind, loving, and respectful—always with good words and works.

*Chapter 9*

Shine your light without hesitation
and others will be inspired to shine, too!
(Unattributed)

# References

*ABC News* (2022). "Trump sues New York AG Letitia James after she sued him for $250M." Retrieved November 3, 2022, from https://www.msn.com/en-us/news/politics/trump-sues-new-york-ag-letitia-james-after-she-sued-him-for-250m/ar-AA13G6tg?cvid=bafa378f5b9b47179e7bf185051fc4e0.

Aguilar, E. & L. Cohen (2022). *The PD Book: 7 Habits That Transform Professional Development.* Hoboken, NJ: John Wiley & Sons, Inc.

Antoinette Oglethorpe Ltd. (2022). *John C. Maxwell quotes.* Retrieved October 24, 2022, from https://www.antoinetteoglethorpe.com/leadership-development-quotes/.

AZQuotes.com (2022a). *Louis Pasteur quotes.* Retrieved October 20, 2022, from https://www.azquotes.com/quotes/topics/tenacity.html.

———. (2022b). *Theodore Roosevelt quotes.* Retrieved November 1, 2022, from https://www.azquotes.com/quotes/topics/obeying-the-law.html.

———. (2022c). *Top 25 quotes by Orrin Woodward.* Retrieved October 1, 2022, from https://www.azquotes.com/author/47506-Orrin_Woodward.

Babcock, C. L. (1991). *A Comparison of Male and Female Elementary School Principals' Perceived Instructional Leadership Behavior.* Dissertations. 2033. Retrieved September 26, 2022, from https://scholarworks.wmich.edu/dissertations/2033.

Berger, C. (2022). "K–12 workers are the most burned out employees in America, and it's a sign the teacher shortage is about to intensify." Retrieved October 18, 2022, from https://fortune.com/2022/06/15/teachers-burnout-workers-quitting-great-resignation/.

Blank, W., J. R. Weitzel, & S. G. Green (1990). "A test of situational leadership theory." *Personnel Psychology, 43,* 579–97.

BrainyQuote.com (2023). *Oprah Winfrey quotes.* Retrieved February 5, 2023, from https://www.brainyquote.com/quotes/oprah_winfrey_133739.

———. (2022a). *Dwight D. Eisenhower quotes.* Retrieved February 5, 2023, from https://www.brainyquote.com/quotes/dwight_d_eisenhower_112052.

———. (2022b). *Edward Gibbon quotes.* Retrieved November 10, 2022, from https://www.brainyquote.com/quotes/edward_gibbon_393556.

Bridges, F. (2017). "Michelle Obama's best advice to young people." Retrieved October 24, 2022, from https://www.forbes.com/sites/francesbridges/2017/05/31/michelle-obamas-best-advice-to-young-people/?sh=7b51a69c5083.

Carroll, M. (2014). "UH study finds print readers recall more than online readers." Retrieved October 16, 2022, from https://uh.edu/news-events/stories/2014/September/091514printvsonline.php.

Cohen, A. (2017). "For those who are set in their ways and afraid of change." Retrieved October 27, 2022, from https://annecohenwrites.com/set-ways-afraid-change/.

Crampton, A. E., et al. (2018). "Meaningful and expansive literacy learning through technology-mediated productions." Retrieved February 21, 2023, from https://doi.org/10.1002/jaal.723.

Daum, K. (2022). "8 critical things every great leader remembers." Retrieved October 31, 2022, from https://www.inc.com/kevin-daum/8-critical-things-every-great-leader-remembers.html.

De Pree, M. (2001). *Called to Serve*. Grand Rapids, MI: Eerdmans Publishing Company.

DeWray, L. (2019). "Absolutes: Concepts and applications." Unpublished class course conversation. Department of Education and Foundations, The University of Texas at El Paso, El Paso, TX.

Dorn, E., et al. (2022). "COVID-19 and education: The lingering effects of unfinished learning." Retrieved October 16, 2022, from htpps://www.mckinsey.com/industries/education/our-insights/covid-19-and-education-the-lingering-effects-of-unfinished-learning.

Driscoll, M. (2023). "12 hot tips for new principals: 21st century leadership, 21st century principals." Retrieved January 29, 2023, from https://thinkstrategicforschools.com/12-tips-for-new-principals/.

Economy, P. (2022). "7 powerful ways to fail better (and succeed sooner)." Retrieved October 31, 2022, from https://www.inc.com/peter-economy/7-ways-to-fail-better-and-succeed-sooner.html.

*Education Week* (2023). "School shootings this year: How many and where?" Retrieved January 29, 2023, from https://www.edweek.org/leadership/school-shootings-this-year-how-many-and-where/2023/01.

Edwards, E. (2023). "CDC says teen girls are caught in an extreme wave of sadness and violence." Retrieved February 14, 2023, from https://www.nbcnews.com/health/health-news/teen-mental-health-cdc-girls-sadness-violence-rcna69964.

Faust, J. E. (1982). "Integrity, the mother of many virtues." Retrieved October 16, 2022, from https://www.churchofjesuschrist.org/study/general-conference/1982/04/integrity-the-mother-of-many-virtues?lang=eng.

Fernandez, C. F. & R. P. Vecchio (1997). "Situational leadership theory revisited: A test of an across-jobs perspective." *Leadership Quarterly, 8*, 67–84.

Fernandez, M. (2013). "Sentence cut in Texas for school official jailed in test scandal" (*New York Times*, December 12). Retrieved November 3, 2022, from https://www.nytimes.com/2013/12/13/us/sentence-cut-in-texas-for-school-official-jailed-in-test-scandal.html.

FocusU (2022). *Vishwas Chavan quotes*. Retrieved October 24, 2022, from https://focusu.com/blog/100-insightful-quotes-on-accountability/.

Frank, K. A. & K. T. Torphy (2019). "Social media, who cares? A dialogue between a millennial and a curmudgeon." *Teacher College Record, 121*(14), 1–24.

Geisel, T. S. (1990). *Oh, the Places You'll Go!* New York: Random House Children's Books.

Gewertz, C. (2021). "Teachers' mental health has suffered in the pandemic. Here's how districts can help." Retrieved December 15, 2022, from https://www.edweek.org/leadership/teachers-mental-health-has-suffered-in-the-pandemic-heres-how-districts-can-help/2021/05.

Glickman, C. D., S. P. Gordon, & J. M. Gordon (2018). *SuperVision and Instructional Leadership: A Developmental Approach*. New York: Pearson Education, Inc.

GoogleQuotes.com (2022a). *Dr. Prem Jagvasi quotes*. Retrieved November 3, 2022, from https://www.google.com/search?q=self-evaluation+quotes&tbm=isch&ved=2ahUKEwj94M2LsZP7AhVgmWoFHWbBBUMQ2-cCegQIABAA&oq=self-evaluation+quotes&gs_lcp=CgNpbWcQAzIFCAAQgAQyBggAEAcQHjIGCAAQBxAeMgYIABAHEB4yBAgAEB4yBggAEAUQHjIGCAAQBRAeMgYIABAIEB4yBggAEAgQHjoECAAQQzoICAAQBRAHEB46CAgAEAgQBxAeUPgRWLAwYME3aABwAHgBgAHPAYgBxQmSAQU4LjQuMZgBAKABAaoBC2d3cy13aXotaW1nwAEB&sclient=img&ei=CGxkY_28GeCyqtsP5oKXmAQ&bih=714&biw=1536.

———. (2022b). *Tony Hsieh and Amy Poehler quotes*. Retrieved September 27, 2022, from https://www.google.com/search?q=Google+quotes.

Grissom, J., A. J. Egalite, & C. A. Lindsay (2021). "How principals affect students and schools: A systematic synthesis of two decades of research." Retrieved October 31, 2022, from http://www.wallacefoundation.org/principalsynthesis.

Hall, W. J., H. C. Dawes, & N. Plocek (2021). "Sexual orientation identity development milestones among lesbians, gay, bisexual, and queer people: A systematic review and meta-analysis." Retrieved September 27, 2022, from https://www.ncbi.nlm.nih.gov/pmc/articles/PMC8581765/.

Hart, J. (2023). "A teacher who quit and took a job at Costco says life is much better now—she has a life, can pay her bills, and finally sleeps at night." Retrieved February 5, 2023, from https://www.msn.com/en-us/money/careersandeducation/a-teacher-who-quit-and-took-a-job-at-costco-says-life-is-much-better-now-%E2%80%94-she-has-a-life-can-pay-her-bills-and-finally-sleeps-at-night/ar-AA16QtMX?li=BBnbfcL.

Hayne, J. (2021). "As Michael Collins drifted above the moon, he held a 'secret terror' for the Apollo 11 mission." Retrieved February 6, 2023, from https://www.abc.net.au/news/2021-04-29/michael-collins-apollo-11-mission-secret-terror/100103584.

Heifetz, R. & M. Linsky (2002). "A survival guide for leaders." Retrieved October 4, 2022, from https://hbr.org/2002/06/a-survival-guide-for-leaders.

Helterbran, V. R. & S. A. Rieg (2004). "Women as school principals: What is the challenge?" *Journal of Women in Educational Leadership, 107*. Retrieved September 26, 2022, from http://digitalcommons.unl.edu/jwel/107.

Hencley, S. P., L. E. McCleary & J. H. McGrath (1970). *The Elementary School Principalship*. New York: Dodd, Mead, & Company.

Hersey, P. & K. H. Blanchard (1997). *The Management of Organizational Behavior*, 3rd ed. Englewood Cliffs, NJ: Prentice Hall.

Hewertson, R. B. (2020). *Hire Right, Fire Right: A Leader's Guide to Finding and Keeping Your Best People*. Lanham, MD: Rowman & Littlefield Publishing Group, Inc.

Hudson-Barr, D. (2004). "How to read a research article." Retrieved October 12, 2022, from https://onlinelibrary.wiley.com/doi/epdf/10.1111/j.1088–145X.2004.00070.x.

Hughes, R. L., R. C. Ginnett, & G. J. Curphy (2021). *Leadership: Enhancing the Lessons of Experience*, 10th ed. New York: McGraw-Hill Education.

Jordan, B. (2022). "6 leadership traps successful leaders avoid." Retrieved October 30, 2022, from https://aboutleaders.com/6-leadership-traps-successful-leaders-avoid/.

Jordan, P. W. & B. Dimarco (2022). "Educators and ESSER: How pandemic spending is reshaping the teaching profession." Retrieved October 16, 2022, from https://www.future-ed.org/wp-content/uploads/2022/10/Educators-and-ESSER-How-Pandemic-Spending-is-Reshaping-the-Teaching-Profession.pdf.

Korn Ferry. (2023). "Experts reveal how culture equals market value." Retrieved February 21, 2023, from https://www.insights@kornferry.com

Krutka, D. G., et al. (2019). "Teaching 'against' social media: Confronting problems of profit in curriculum." *Teachers College Record, 121*(140310).

Kuhfeld, M., et al. (2022). "The pandemic has had devastating impacts on learning: What will it take to help students catch up?" Retrieved October 16, 2022, from https://www.brookings.edu/blog/brown-center-chalkboard/2022/03/03/the-pandemic-has-had-devastating-impacts-on-learning-what-will-it-take-to-help-students-catch-up/.

Levin, K. & E. Bakuli (2022). "Not 'present,' and paying a steep cost." Retrieved November 14, 2022, from https://detroit.chalkbeat.org/2022/11/7/23422689/school-attendance-detroit-michigan-students-chronic-absenteeism.

Levin, S. & K. Bradley (2019). *Understanding and Addressing Principal Turnover: A Review of the Research*. Reston, VA: National Association of Secondary School Principals.

Lieberman, M. (2023). "COVID relief funds dry up next year: Here's how districts can cope." Retrieved January 22, 2023, from https://www.edweek.org/leadership/covid-relief-funds-dry-up-next-year-heres-how-districts-can-cope/2023/01.

Luperon, A. (2022, November 13). "White teacher put on administrative leave for telling students 'My race is the superior one.'" Retrieved November 14, 2022, from https://lawandcrime.com/high-profile/white-teacher-put-on-administrative-leave-for-telling-students-my-race-is-the-superior-one/.

Marzano, R. J., et al. (2021). *Improving Teacher Development & Evaluation: A Guide for Leaders, Coaches & Teachers*. Bloomington, IN: Marzano Resources.

Master Teacher, The (2018). "When there's a disconnect between district and site agendas." Retrieved December 15, 2022, from https://masterteacher.net/disconnect-between-district-and-site-agendas/.

McConnel, S. (2017). "Stephanie McConnel of Principal Principles." Retrieved December 20, 2023, from https://www.teacherspayteachers.com/Store/Stephanie-Mcconnell-Of-Principal-Principles.

McIntosh, C. (2006). "What's your power style?" *Essence* (October).

McIntyre, M. (2022). "The inclusive school." Retrieved December 15, 2022, from https://www.greatschools.org/gk/articles/the-inclusive-school/.

McKibben, S. (2015). "The principal as lead learner." Retrieved October 16, 2022, from https://www.ascd.org/el/articles/the-principal-as-lead-learner.

McLuhan, M. (2010). *The Medium and the Light: Reflections on Religion and Media*. Eugene, OR: Wipf & Amp 80. 4.

McPeake, J. A. (2007). "The Principalship: A study of the principal's time on task from 1960 to the twenty-first century." Theses, Dissertations and Capstones. Paper 765. Retrieved September 26, 2022, from https://mds.marshall.edu/cgi/viewcontent.cgi?article=1726&context=etd.

Merrick, C. (2020). "10 things highly successful leaders must forget and never do." Retrieved October 31, 2022, from https://carenmerrick.com/leadership-qualities-10-things-leaders-should-never-do/.

Miller, M. (2022). "The great resignation and what it means for the future of teaching." Retrieved October 18, 2022, from https://studybreaks.com/college/the-great-resignation-teaching/.

———. (1982). *Lyndon: An Oral Biography*. New York: Putnam Publishing Group.

Mineo, L. (2022). "'Shadow pandemic' of domestic violence." Retrieved February 14, 2023, from https://news.harvard.edu/gazette/story/2022/06/shadow-pandemic-of-domestic-violence/.

Mungal, A. S. & R. D. Sorenson (2020). *Steps to Success: What Successful Principals Do Every Day*. Lanham, MD: Rowman & Littlefield Publishing Group, Inc.

Najarro, I. (2022, November 3). "How is white superiority embedded in school systems today? A scholar explains." Retrieved November 11, 2022, from https://www.edweek.org/leadership/how-is-white-superiority-embedded-in-school-systems-today-a-scholar-explains/2022/11.

National Association of School Psychologists (NASP) (2021). "Responding to school violence: Tips for administrators." Retrieved February 5, 2023, from https://www.nasponline.org/resources-and-publications/resources-and-podcasts/school-safety-and-crisis/school-violence-resources/school-violence-prevention/responding-to-school-violence-tips-for-administrators.

National Association of Secondary School Principals (NASSP) (2022). "NASSP school safety resources." Retrieved February 5, 2023, from https://www.nassp.org/nassp-school-safety-resources/.

National Council for Education Statistics (2020). "Characteristics of public school principals." Retrieved February 15, 2023, from https://nces.ed.gov/programs/coe/indicator/cls/public-school-principals.

National Student Support Accelerator (2021). "Toolkit for Tutoring Programs." Retrieved February 28, 2023, from https://doi.org/10.26300/5n7h-mh59.

Northouse, P. G. (2021). *Leadership: Theory and Practice*. Los Angeles: Sage Publications, Inc.

Norton, M. S. (2017). *Guiding the Human Resources Function in Education*. Lanham, MD: Rowman & Littlefield Publishing Group, Inc.

———. (2015). *The Principal as Human Resources Leader: A Guide to Exemplary Practices for Personnel Administration*. Lanham, MD: Rowman & Littlefield Publishing Group, Inc.

Novotney, A. (2019). "The risk of social isolation." Retrieved February 15, 2023, from https://www.apa.org/monitor/2019/05/ce-corner-isolation.

Peetz, C. (2022). "The status of the teaching profession is at a 50-year low: What can we do about it?" Retrieved December 15, 2022, from https://www.edweek.org/teaching-learning/the-status-of-the-teaching-profession-is-at-a-50-year-low-what-can-we-do-about-it/2022/11#:~:text=Multiple%20data%20sources%20confirm%20the%20findings&text=Interest%20in%20the%20teaching%20profession,and%2038%20percent%20since%202010.

Porter, R. & S. Hezlett (2023). "The top 5 career stoppers and stallers." Retrieved January 26, 2023, from https://www.kornferry.com/insights/this-week-in-leadership/the-top-five-career-stoppers-and-stallers.

Portnoy, G. & J. Hart-Angelo (1983). "Cheers lyrics: Where everybody knows your name." Retrieved November 1, 2022, from https://www.stlyrics.com/lyrics/televisiontvthemelyrics-80s90s/cheers.htm.

Positive Action (2022). "How to create a positive school culture and climate." Retrieved October 27, 2022, from https://www.positiveaction.net/positive-school-climate-culture.

Querolo, N., O. Rockeman, & E. Ceron (2022). "Part 1: Why teachers are quitting." Retrieved October 18, 2022, from https://www.bloomberg.com/features/2022-america-teachers-great-resignation/?leadSource=uverify%20wall.

QuotesCover.com (2012–2021). "51 mistake quotes to get you inspired." Retrieved November 1, 2022, from https://quotescover.com/topics/mistake.

QuoteFancy.com (2022a). *George Washington quotes*. Retrieved November 28, 2022, from https://quotefancy.com/quote/816943/George-Washington-We-must-never-despair-our-situation-has-been-compromising-before-and-it.

———. (2022b). *Mushfiqur Rahim quotes*. Retrieved October 24, 2022, from https://quotefancy.com/quote/1784031/Mushfiqur-Rahim-The-more-the-responsibility-and-expectations-on-me-the-more-I-like-it-I.

QuoteHD.com (2022). *Michael Polzin quotes*. Retrieved November 1, 2022, from http://www.quotehd.com/quotes/michael-polzin-quote-we-have-to-follow-the-law-we-dont-have-a-choice-in-this.

Ramanathan, S. (2019). "10 keys to personal growth." Retrieved October 4, 2022, from https://maximisepotential.blogspot.com/2016/11/10-keys-to-personal-growth.html.

Rose, L. (n.d.). "Inclusive school leadership." Retrieved December 15, 2022, from https://inclusiveschoolcommunities.org.au/resources/toolkit/inclusive-school-leadership.

Ruggirello, A. (2022). "New research points to a continuing principal shortage." Retrieved October 1, 2022, from https://www.wallacefoundation.org/news-and-media/blog/pages/new-research-points-to-a-looming-principal-shortage.aspx.

Sharp, W. L. & J. K. Walter (2012). *The Principal as School Manager*. Lanham, MD: Rowman & Littlefield Education.

Sorenson, R. D. (2023). "Dumpster fires: Tales, trials, and tribulations of new principals." Unpublished interviews. Department of Educational Leadership and Foundations, The University of Texas at El Paso, El Paso, TX.

———. (2012). "Organizational climate and culture." Course PowerPoint and class discussion. Department of Educational Leadership and Foundations, The University of Texas at El Paso, El Paso, TX.

———. (2010). "A great educator speaks to the significance of climate and culture in schools, today." Unpublished conversation. Department of Educational Leadership and Foundations, The University of Texas at El Paso, El Paso, TX.

———. (2002). "The novice principal: How to avoid the pitfalls leading to career derailment." *Texas Study of Secondary Education, XII*(1), 28–31.

Sorenson, R. D. & L. M. Goldsmith (2021). "Art Linkletter was right: Kids do say the darndest things." Unpublished journal article. Department of Educational Leadership and Foundations, The University of Texas at El Paso, El Paso, TX.

———. (2009). *The Principal's Guide to Managing School Personnel*. Thousand Oaks, CA: Corwin.

Sorenson, R. D., L. M. Goldsmith, & D. E. DeMatthews (2016). *The Principal's Guide to Time Management: Instructional Leadership in the Digital Age*. Thousand Oaks, CA: Corwin.

Sparks, S. D. (2022). "Pandemic anxiety was higher for teachers than for health-care workers." Retrieved December 15, 2022, from https://www.edweek.org/teaching-learning/pandemic-anxiety-was-higher-for-teachers-than-for-health-care-workers/2022/11?s_kwcid=AL!6416!3!602270476281!!!g!!&utm_source=goog&utm_medium=cpc&utm_campaign=ew+dynamic+recent&ccid=dynamic+ads+recent+articles&ccag=recent+articles+dynamic&cckw=&cccv=dynamic+ad&gclid=EAIaIQobChMIkbLespn8-wIVTBTUAR2VPwnNEAAYASAAEgIlOPD_BwE.

Stebbins, S. (2023, February). "Here's how many guns were sold in Texas last month." Retrieved February 24, 2023, from https://www.msn.com/en-us/money/markets/here-s-how-many-guns-were-sold-in-texas-last-month/ar-AA17TLT8?ocid=hpmsn&cvid=4f76e155ab27475cbce5173fd3891dbc.

Subramanyam, R. V. (2013). "Art of reading a journal article: Methodically and effectively." Retrieved October 12, 2022, from https://www.ncbi.nlm.nih.gov/pmc/articles/PMC3687192/#:~:text=Reading%20scientific%20literature%20is%20a,in%20designing%20one's%20research%20project.

Superville, D. R. (2023). "Is this the beginning of the principal exodus?" Retrieved February 25, 2023, from https://www.edweek.org/leadership/is-this-the-beginning-of-the-principal-exodus/2023/02?utm_source=nl&utm_medium=eml&utm_campaign=popweek&utm_content=list&M=6255417&UUID=14f3b062c0baef467fd6eefe3a4d6cd4&T=8400124.

TASB.org (2022). "School board policy versus regulation: What's the difference?" Retrieved November 3, 2022, from https://www.tasb.org/members/enhance-district/school-board-policy-and-regulation.aspx#:~:text=Policies%20define%20the%20purposes%20and,what%20it%20wants%20of%20administration.

Vamboa.org (2022). "65 famous quotes." Retrieved October 4, 2022, from https://vamboa.org/65-famous-quotes-from-famous-people-on-failure-to-motivate-you-for-success/.

Wallace Foundation, J. A. Grissom, A. J. Egalite, & C. A. Lindsay (2021). "How principals affect students and schools: A systematic synthesis of two decades of research." Retrieved October 27, 2022, from https://www.wallacefoundation.org/knowledge-center/pages/how-principals-affect-students-and-schools-a-systematic-synthesis-of-two-decades-of-research.aspx?PF=1.

Will, M. (2022). "Stress, burnout, depression: Teachers and principals are not doing well, new data confirm." Retrieved November 15, 2022, from https://www.edweek.org/teaching-learning/stress-burnout-depression-teachers-and-principals-are-not-doing-well-new-data-confirm/2022/06?s_kwcid=AL!6416!3!602270476281!!!g!!&utm_source=goog&utm_medium=cpc&utm_campaign=ew+dynamic+recent&ccid=dynamic+ads+recent+articles&ccag=recent+articles+dynamic&cckw=&cccv=dynamic+ad&gclid=EAIaIQobChMI_Yr6i7ix-wIVrBvUAR0jkQCEEAAYASAAEgJb4_D_BwE.

———. (2019). "4 things principals can do (and 4 things they shouldn't) to build relationships with teachers." Retrieved October 31, 2022, from https://www.edweek.org/leadership/4-things-principals-can-do-and-4-things-they-shouldnt-to-build-relationships-with-teachers/2019/10.

Yukl, G. A. & W. L. Gardner III (2019). *Leadership in Organizations*. Upper Saddle River, NJ: Pearson Education, Inc.

Zalaznick, M. (2022). "More activist parents aren't going away: Here's how to work with them." Retrieved October 18, 2022, from https://districtadministration.com/more-activist-parents-arent-going-away-heres-how-to-work-with-them/.

Zippa, Inc. (2022a). "Principal demographics and statistics in the U.S." Retrieved September 26, 2022, from https://www.zippia.com/assistant-principal-jobs/dem.

———. (2022b). "School principal demographics and statistics in the U.S." Retrieved September 26, 2022, from https://www.zippia.com/school-principal-jobs/demographics/.

# Index

absolute #1, lead learner principal, 36
absolute #2, instructional leadership: adaptation challenges, 39; overview, 37; program supervision and evaluation, 38; special education and inclusive school, 37–38
absolute #3, leadership team assembly, 39–40
absolute #4, school personnel supervision: challenges, 40; engagement with teacher resisters, 42–43; helping teachers in need of assistance, 41–42; interaction with best teachers, 41; management of personnel and adverse circumstances, 43; overview, 40; supervision of marginal teachers, 42; teacher mental health issues, 41, 53, 56
absolute #5, school operations management, 44
absolute #6, school safety and security, 44–45
absolute #7, enduring emergent forces: activist parents, 57–58; adaptability to, 52; case study application, 67–68; controversial issues, 61–66, 67; discussion questions, 66–67; incivility, lack of public decorum and survival tactics, 58–60; overview, 45, 51–52, 66; pandemic aftereffects, 52–54; social media effects, 61; teacher shortages, quiet quitting and Great Resignation, 54–56; technology redefined, 60
absolutes, leadership: overview, 36, 46; recognizing and knowing, xiii–xiv, 35–36. *See also specific absolutes*
adaptation: challenges for new principal, 39; challenges in instructional leadership, 39; as key skill, 75–76
administrative regulations, 123, 124–25
Aldrin, Buzz, 29
American Rescue Plan (2021), 53
Armstrong, Neil, 29
attributes, new principal personal: ascertaining crucial, 19; leadership protocol, 129–34; overview, xv
attributes of successful new principals: acquiring essential skills, traits and characteristics, 9; incorporating school district policies, regulations and procedures, 11–12; learning role expectations and responsibilities, 8–9; overview, 6–8, 12; understanding school norms and traditions, 9–10; valuing essential facets of learning community, 10–11

"Baker's Dozen" list, 58

Brookings Institute, 52
Brown Center, 52

Cannibals at School scenario, 105, 106
career pitfalls, 93–94
Centers for Disease Control and Prevention (CDC), 53
challenges, new principal: adaptation, 39; as overwhelming, 112; school personnel supervision, 40
"change when change is not required" pitfall, 94
Chavan, Vishwas, 73
*Cheers*, 110
Cohen, Anne, 85
collective we, 22–23
Collins, Michael, 29
combination leadership profile, 133
communication skills: active communication with learning community, 109; enhancement of, 19
community members, 103–4. *See also* learning community members
conferences: educational, 24; presentations at, 28–29
conflict recognition, 24
controversial issues, 61–66, 67
COVID-19 pandemic: aftereffects, 52–54; as emergent force, 52–54; principal resignations and retirements post, xi.xii
critical leadership skills: acquisition of, 21–25; attribute of acquiring, 9; case study application, 32–34; discussion questions, 32; identification of, 20–21; overcoming of isolation, 29–31; overview, xiii, 31–32; personal growth and development, 25–29; plan of action development, 17–20
Curphy, G. J., 9

decisiveness, as key skill, 76

dedicated leadership profile, 133
DeMatthews, D. E., 25, 26, 111
De Pree, Max, 69
DeWray, LuRella, 35
Diamond, John, 62, 64
diplomatic leadership profile, 133
Dorn, E., 53
driven leadership profile, 132–33

educational conferences, 24
educational laws: finance scenario, 119; overview, 118; romance scenario, 118, 120–21; school board policies and, 121. *See also* legal responsibilities, of new principal
Egalite, A. J., 107
Einstein, Albert, 110
Eisenhower, Dwight D., 118
Elementary and Secondary School Emergency Relief (ESSER III), 54
*The Elementary School Principalship* (Hencley, McCleary, McGrath), 1–2
ELLs. *See* English language learners
emergent forces: activist parents, 57–58; adaptability to, 52; controversial issues, 61–66, 67; incivility, lack of public decorum and survival tactics, 58–60; overview, 45, 51–52, 66; pandemic aftereffects, 52–54; social media effects, 61; teacher shortages, quiet quitting and Great Resignation, 54–56; technology redefined, 60
emotional growth, 27
empathy, as key skill, 76
endurance, as key skill, 76–77
English language learners (ELLs), 54
equity, as key skill, 76
*Equity, Equality, and Empathy* (Sorenson), 27, 76
ESSER III. *See* Elementary and Secondary School Emergency Relief
expectations, of new principal, xiv, 70–72, 78; differences between responsibilities and, 73–75; role expectations, 4–5, 6, 8–9

Faust, James E., 35, 36
federal funding, 54
female new principal, of today and yesteryear, 5
Fortune 500 companies, 25
Frank, K. A., 61

Gallop Poll, 54
Gault, Stanley, 88
Geisel, Theodor Seuss, 87
Gewertz, C., 41
Gibbon, Edward, 28
Ginnett, R. C., 9
Goldsmith, L. M., 9, 25, 26, 30, 42, 111; *The Principal's Guide to Managing School Personnel*, 43, 121
Great Resignation, xii, 54–56
Grissom, J. A., 107

Heifetz, R., 59–60
help: new principals asking for, 25; overcoming failure through helpfulness, 111; for teachers in need of assistance, 41–42
Hencley, Stephen P., 1–2
honesty, overcoming failure through, 111
Hsieh, Tony, 11
Hudson-Barr, D., 27
Hughes, R. L., 9
humor, incorporation of good, 30

incivility, 58–60
inclusive school, 37–38
indecisive pitfall, 95
inspirational principals, 23–24
institutional change, 89–90
instructional coaches, 103
instructional leadership: adaptation challenges, 39; overview, 37; *The Principal's Guide to Time Management*, 26, 77; program supervision and evaluation, 38; special education and inclusive school, 37–38

interpersonal skills, as key skill, 76
isolation, overcoming of, 29–31

Jagvasi, Prem, 129
James, Letitia, 119
Johnson, Lyndon B., 94
justice, appliance of, 117–18

key skills, 75–77, 94, 108–10
Krutka, D. G., 61

laws: educational, 118–21; obeying of, 117–18
leaderless pitfall, 93
*Leadership* (Hughes, Ginnett, Curphy), 9
leadership absolutes. *See* absolutes, leadership
leadership protocol, 129–34
leadership styles: primary, 24–25; profiles, 132–34
leadership team assembly, 39–40
lead-learner, 24, 25
lead learner principal, 36
learning community: active communication with, 109; *Equity, Equality, and Empathy*, 27, 76; essential characteristics, 105–7; fundamental factors impacting new principal's relationship with, xv, 107; how to not build relationship with, 116–18; key tenets of great first impressions with, 109–10; key tenets to establishing effective, xv; LLCs, 101–2; overview, 101–5; PLCs, 101; rapport development and relationship establishment, 108–09; valuing essential facets of, 10–11. *See also* new principal success, Step #5, learning community characteristics
learning community members: new principals' position responsibilities as, 104–5; overview, 102–4; position importance, 105; roles and responsibilities, 102–4

legal responsibilities, of new principal: administrative regulations, 123, 124–25; campus procedures, 123–24, 125; overview, xv, 118, 124–25; school board policies, 121–23, 124–25; school personnel supervision and, 123; school superintendent and, 122
LGBTQ+, 39
LGBTQ+ new principals, of today and yesteryear, 6
Lindsay, C. A., 107
Linsky, M., 59–60
listening, as learning, 24
local learning communities (LLCs), 101–2. *See also* learning community

male new principal, of today and yesteryear, 5
Maltz, Maxwell, 110
Maxwell, John C., 69
McClearly, Lloyd E., 1–2
McConnel, Stephanie, xi
McGrath, J. H., 1–2
McKibben, S., 36
McLuhan, Marshall, 60
Méndez, Zulma, 93
mental growth, 26
mental health issues, of teachers, 41, 53, 56
mentor, 27, 30
Millay, Edna St. Vincent, 111

NASP. *See* National Association of School Psychologists
NASSP. *See* National Association of Secondary School Principals
*NASSP School Safety Resources* (NASSP), 45
National Association of School Psychologists (NASP), 45
National Association of Secondary School Principals (NASSP), xii, 45
National Center for Education Statistics (NCES), xii, 54

networking, with other principals, 24, 30
never-seen pitfall, 94
new principal, xi; behaviors, 87–88; female, 5; ill-equipped, xii–xiii; never despair, 135; preparation, 109, 135; recruitment and retainment of, xiii; shining your light, 135–36; social issues awareness, 135. *See also specific topics*
new principal, of today: aspects, 2–3; demographics, 5; discussion questions, 13; female, 5; functions, 3, 5, 6; LGBTQ+, 6; male, 5; new principal of yesteryear compared to, 2–6, 12, 13; role expectations, 4–5, 6; student management, 3, 5
new principal, of yesteryear: aspects, 2–3; case study application, 13–15; demographics, 5; discussion questions, 13; female, 5; functions, 3, 5, 6, 12; LGBTQ+, 6; male, 5; new principal of today compared to, 2–6, 12, 13; overview, 1–3, 12; role expectations, 4–5, 6; student management, 3, 5
new principal success: administrative role, xiii; overview of steps to, xiii–xiv, 134
new principal success, Step #1, critical leadership skills: acquisition of critical leadership skills, 21–25; case study application, 32–34; discussion questions, 32; identification of critical leadership skills, 20–21; overcoming of isolation, 29–31; overview, xiii, 31–32; personal growth and development, 25–29; plan of action development, 17–20
new principal success, Step #2, essential leadership absolutes: case study application, 47–50; discussion questions, 46–47; overview, xiii–xiv, 46. *See also* absolutes, leadership

new principal success, Step #3, expectations, responsibilities and skills: case study application, 80–82; discussion questions, 79; expectations, 70–72, 73–75, 78; making of outstanding new principal, 77–78, 79; overview, xiv, 78–79; responsibilities, 72–75, 78–79; skills, 75–77, 78

new principal success, Step #4, norms, traditions, customs: career longevity, 93–94; case study application, 96–99; changing climate, culture and, 92–93; discussion questions, 95–96; essential knowledge and understanding, 85–86; institutional changes principals can make to, 87–88; institutional perpetuation of, 86–87; overview, xiv, 83–84, 94–95; school climate and culture dictated by, 88–91; surviving changes to, 91–93

new principal success, Step #5, learning community characteristics: case study application, 114–16; discussion questions, 112–14; essential characteristics, 105–7; fundamental factors impacting relationship, xv, 107; how to not build relationship, 114–16; key tenets of great first impressions, 109–10; learning community overview, 101–5; overview, xiv–xv, 102–3, 112; position responsibilities, 104–5; rapport development, relationship establishment, 108–10; success through failure, 110–12

new principal success, Step #6, legal responsibilities: administrative regulations, 123, 124–25; campus procedures, 123–24, 125; case study application, 126–27; discussion questions, 125–26; overview, xv, 118, 124–25; school board policies, 121–23, 124–25

new principal success, Step #7, personal attributes: leadership protocol, 129–34; overview, xv
Northouse, P. G., 9

Obama, Michelle, 77
*Oh, the Places You'll Go!* (Geisel), 87
open-door policy, 109–10
organization, as essential, 26

pandemic. *See* COVID-19 pandemic
parents: activist, 57–58; as learning community members, 103
personal attributes, new principal: ascertaining crucial, 19; leadership protocol, 129–34; overview, xv
personal growth and development, new principal: keys to, 25–29; presentations at conferences in, 28–29; research literature in, 27–28; writing for publications in, 29
personnel management: of adverse circumstances, 43; *The Principal's Guide to Managing School Personnel*, 43, 121
physical growth, 27
pilot programs, 111
plan of action development, new principal: ascertaining crucial personal attributes, 19; enhancement of communication skills, 19; identifying and advancing leadership skills, 18–19; overview, 17–18, 19–20; pinpointing of necessary self-management skills, 19; recognition of decision-making and problem-solving skills to possess, 19
PLCs. *See* professional learning communities
Poehler, Amy, 11
political issues, 39
Polzin, Michael, 117
Positive Action, 92

principals: *The Elementary School Principalship*, 1–2; *Equity, Equality, and Empathy*, 27, 76; inspirational, 23–24; lead learner, 36; as learning community members, 103; NASSP, xii, 45; networking with other, 24, 30; postpandemic era resignations and retirements, xi, xii; *Responding to Resisters*, 19, 43; working from home, xi. *See also* new principal
*The Principal's Guide to Managing School Personnel* (Sorenson and Goldsmith), 43, 121
*The Principal's Guide to Time Management* (Sorenson), 26, 77
professional learning communities (PLCs), 101
programs: pilot, 109; supervision and evaluation, 38
publications, writing for, 29

questions, accepting and answering, 110
quiet quitting, 54–56

racism, 62–65
Rahim, Mushfiqur "Mr. Dependable," 69
Ramanthan, S., 25
RAND Corporation, xii, 41, 55, 56
Remember This; Don't Do That!, 112, *113*
resiliency, overcoming failure through, 111–12
resisters, 42–43
resource management, 107
*Responding to Resisters* (Sorenson), 19, 43
*Responding to School Violence* (NASP), 45
responsibilities, 104
responsibilities, of new principal: attribute of learning, 8–9; differences between expectations and, 73–75; learning community member position responsibilities, 104–5; overview, 72–73, 78–79; roles and, 102–4; school superintendent's delegation of new, 131–32. *See also* legal responsibilities, of new principal
risk taking, 26
role expectations, of new principal: attribute of learning, 8–9; of yesteryear and today, 4–5, 6
Roosevelt, Theodore, 117

Santana, Arthur D., 58, 59
school: campus procedures, 123–24, 125; federal funding, 54; operations management, 44; safety and security, 44–45; shootings, 44–45
school administrators: administrative regulations, 123, 124–25; district administrators, 104; school board policies and, 121
school board, activist parents and, 57, 58
school board policies, 11; case study application, 126–27; educational laws and, 121; legal responsibilities of new principal and, 121–23, 124–25; school administrators and, 121; school coaches and, 126–27
school climate: changing and improving, 89–91; changing norms, traditions, customs by changing, 92–93; establishment of productive and positive, 88, 90, 107; overview, 88–89; school norms, traditions, customs dictating, 88–91
school coaches, school board policies and, 126–27
school culture: changing and improving, 89–91; changing norms, traditions, customs by changing, 92–93; establishment of open, 88, 90, 107; overview, 89; school norms, traditions, customs dictating, 89–91
school customs: changing climate, culture and, 92–93; essential

knowledge and understanding, 85–86; institutional changes principals can make to, 87–88; institutional perpetuation of, 86–87; overview, xiv, 83–84; school climate and culture dictated by, 88–91; surviving changes to, 91–93
school district: administrators, 104; interactions with leaders of, 30–31; policies, 11–12
school norms: attribute of understanding, 9–10; changing climate, culture and, 92–93; essential knowledge and understanding, 85–86; institutional changes principals can make to, 87–88; institutional perpetuation of, 86–87; overview, xiv, 83–84; school climate and culture dictated by, 88–91; surviving changes to, 91–93
school personnel supervision: campus procedures, 124; challenges, 40; engagement with teacher resisters, 42–43; helping teachers in need of assistance, 41–42; interaction with best teachers, 41; legal responsibilities of new principal and, 123; management of personnel and adverse circumstances, 43; overview, 40; supervision of marginal teachers, 42; teacher mental health issues, 41, 53, 56
school traditions: attribute of understanding, 9–10; changing climate, culture and, 94–95; essential knowledge and understanding, 85–86; institutional changes principals can make to, 87–88; institutional perpetuation of, 86–87; overview, xiv, 83–84; school climate and culture dictated by, 88–91; surviving changes to, 91–93
Sears, Roebuck and Company, 41
*Secondary School Administration* (Hencley, McCleary), 1–2

SEL. *See* Social and Emotional Learning
self care, 26
self-confidence, as key skill, 77
self-discipline, 22
self-evaluation and reflection, 26
7 Bs to overcoming failure in order to succeed, 111–12
Sharp, W. L., 44
situational awareness, 23
skills, leadership, 78; keys to development of, 75–77. *See also* critical leadership skills
Social and Emotional Learning (SEL), 54
social growth, 27
social issues, 39
social issues awareness, 135
social media, 61
social mores, 39
soft skills, 24
Sorenson, R. D., 9, 25, 30, 42, 88, 90, 93, 111; *Equity, Equality, and Empathy*, 27, 76; *The Principal's Guide to Managing School Personnel*, 43, 121; *The Principal's Guide to Time Management*, 26, 77; *Responding to Resisters*, 19, 43
special education, 37–38
spiritual growth, 27
staff, school: learning names quickly of, 110; suggestions or recommendations from, 109
students: attendance and absenteeism, 53; differences, 37; as learning community members, 103; unfinished learning, 53
Subramanyam, R. V., 27
superintendent, school: delegation of new responsibilities to principal by, 131–32; legal responsibilities of new principal and, 122
supervisors, reaching out to, 30
support: overcoming failure through, 111; for teachers, 55–56

survival guide for success, 59–60

teachers: achieving buy-in and commitment of, 108; best, 41; best practices, 36; building relationships with, 108; healthcare plans, 56; ignoring veteran, 108; as learning community members, 103; learning names quickly of, 110; marginal, 42; mental health issues, 41, 53, 56; motivation of, 71–72; in need of assistance, 41–42; principal engagement with, 107; principal facilitation of productive collaboration with, 107; racism of, 63–65; as resisters, 42–43; shortages, 54–56; suggestions or recommendations from, 109; support for, 55–56
technology, education and, 60
timeliness, overcoming failure through, 111

time management, 26, 77
Torphy, K. T., 61

uninformed pitfall, 94

visibility, as key skill, 76, 94, 108–9

Waitley, Denis, 110–11
Wallace Foundation, 87
*Wall Street Journal*, 44
Walter, J. K., 44
Washington, George, 135
watchfulness, overcoming failure through, 111–12
white superiority, 62–65
Will, M., 108
Winfrey, Oprah, 51
Woodward, Orrin, 17, 20

Zalaznick, M., 58

# About the Author

**Dr. Richard D. Sorenson**, professor emeritus, resides in Cypress (northwest Houston), Texas. He is the former director of the Principal Preparation Program and chairperson of the Educational Leadership and Foundations Department at the University of Texas at El Paso (UTEP). Dr. Sorenson earned his doctorate from Texas A&M University at Corpus Christi. He served for twenty-five years as a social studies teacher, assistant principal, principal, and associate superintendent for human resources.

Dr. Sorenson has worked with graduate students at UTEP in the areas of school-based budgeting, personnel, educational law, and leadership development. He was previously named the University of Texas at El Paso College of Education Professor of the Year.

Dr. Sorenson is an active writer, with numerous professional journal publications. He has authored eleven principal leadership textbooks, as well as teacher resource guides and student workbooks. He has been actively involved in numerous professional organizations, including the Texas Elementary Principals and Supervisors Association and the Texas Association of Secondary School Principals, for which he conducted annual new-principal academy seminars.

Dr. Sorenson has been married to his wife and best friend, Donna, for the past forty-seven years and they have two adult children, Lisa (son-in-law, Sam) and Ryan (daughter-in-law, Nataly), and four young grandchildren, Savannah, Nehemiah Amelia, and Oliver—all of whom are the pride and joy of his life.

www.ingramcontent.com/pod-product-compliance
Lightning Source LLC
Chambersburg PA
CBHW032027230426
43671CB00005B/220